## English for international communication
## Jack C. Richards

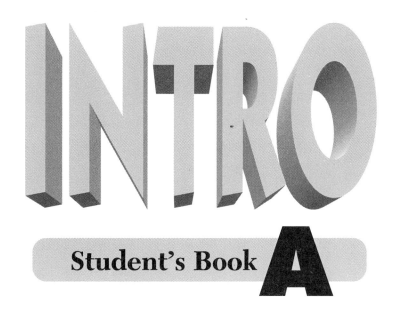

Student's Book **A**

**CAMBRIDGE**
UNIVERSITY PRESS

Published by the Press Syndicate of the University of Cambridge
The Pitt Building, Trumpington Street, Cambridge CB2 1RP
40 West 20th Street, New York, NY 10011-4211, USA
10 Stamford Road, Oakleigh, Melbourne, Australia

© Cambridge University Press 1994

First published 1994
Second printing 1995

Printed in the United States of America

*Library of Congress Cataloging-in-Publication Data*
Richards, Jack C.
Interchange : English for international communication : intro
student's book / Jack C. Richards.
p. cm.
ISBN 0-521-46744-6
1. English language - Textbooks for foreign speakers.
2. Communication. International - Problems, exercises, etc.
I. Title.  II. Title: Intro student's book.
PE1128.R456   1994                          94-17933
428.2´4 - dc20                              CIP


ISBN 0 521 46744 6    Intro Student's Book
ISBN 0 521 46742 X    Intro Teacher's Manual
ISBN 0 521 46743 8    Intro Workbook
ISBN 0 521 46741 1    Intro Class Cassettes

*Split editions:*
ISBN 0 521 47185 0    Intro Student's Book A
ISBN 0 521 47186 9    Intro Student's Book B
ISBN 0 521 47187 7    Intro Workbook A
ISBN 0 521 47188 5    Intro Workbook B
ISBN 0 521 46740 3    Intro Student Cassette A
ISBN 0 521 47189 3    Intro Student Cassette B

Book design: Peter Ducker
Layout and design services: Adventure House, McNally Graphic Design
Cover design: Tom Wharton

Illustrators:
Randy Jones
Mark Kaufman
Beth McNally
Wally Neibart
Eva Sakmar-Sullivan
Bill Thomson
Sam Viviano

# Contents

# Plan of Intro Book A

| | | Topics | Functions | Grammar |
|---|---|---|---|---|
| UNIT | 1 | **Topics** Alphabet; greetings and leave-takings; titles of address; classroom objects; telephone numbers | **Functions** Introducing yourself; spelling names and words; saying phone numbers; giving classroom instructions | **Grammar** Possessive adjectives *my, your, his,* and *her;* the verb *be:* affirmative statements and contractions; numbers 1–10; articles *a* and *an;* imperatives (affirmative) |
| UNIT | 2 | **Topics** Personal items, possessions, and locations in a room | **Functions** Naming objects; finding the owner of an item; asking for and giving location | **Grammar** Plurals; *this* and *these;* possessive of names; possessive adjectives; the verb *be:* yes/no questions and short answers with *it* and *they;* prepositions of place |
| UNIT | 3 | **Topics** Countries; regions; nationalities; languages | **Functions** Asking for and giving information about country of origin, nationality, native language, and geographical locations | **Grammar** Affirmative and negative statements with *be;* adjectives of nationality; questions and short answers with *be* |
| UNIT | 4 | **Topics** Clothing, colors; weather, temperatures, and seasons of the year | **Functions** Asking about and describing clothing; talking about current activities; talking about the weather | **Grammar** Present continuous: affirmative and negative statements; numbers to 100; adjectives after *be* |

## Review of Units 1–4

| | | | | |
|---|---|---|---|---|
| UNIT | 5 | **Topics** Times of the day, clock time; daily activities; Saturday chores | **Functions** Asking for and telling time; asking about and describing current activities | **Grammar** Present continuous: *what + doing,* yes/no questions and short answers; Wh-questions; adverbs of time |
| UNIT | 6 | **Topics** Transportation; family relationships; daily habits; days of the week | **Functions** Asking for and giving information about where you live, how you go to work, and what you do every day | **Grammar** Present tense: affirmative and negative statements; third-person singular endings; irregular verbs and yes/no and Wh-questions; present time expressions |
| UNIT | 7 | **Topics** Homes; rooms; furniture | **Functions** Asking about and describing different homes; saying what furniture is in a room | **Grammar** Present tense: yes/no questions and short answers; *There's /There are* and *There's no/There aren't any* |
| UNIT | 8 | **Topics** Occupations; places of work; salaries | **Functions** Asking and giving information about what people do, where they work, and how they like their jobs | **Grammar** Present tense: Wh-questions with *do;* descriptive adjectives; placement of adjectives before nouns |

## Review of Units 5–8

## Interchange Activities

# Acknowledgments

## Text Credits

**2** *The Cambridge Encyclopedia* © 1990 Cambridge University Press.
**14** "The Immigrants," *Business Week,* 13 July 1992.
**18** *The Cambridge Encyclopedia* © 1990 Cambridge University Press.
**20** *Curious Customs: The Stories Behind 296 Popular American Rituals* by Tad Tuleja © 1987 by The Stonesong Press.
**36** "New Frontiers in Commuting," *Fortune,* 13 January 1992.
**51** "The Best Jobs in America," *Money,* March 1994.

## Illustrators

Randy Jones 6 *(bottom),* 22 *(top),* 24, 31, 33 *(bottom),* 48, 49 *(top),* 54, IC–9, IC–11
Mark Kaufman 6 *(top),* 9 *(all),* 11 *(all),* 12 *(bottom),* 28, 45, IC–3
Beth McNally 12 *(middle)*
Wally Neibart 7, 23, 26, 29, 30 *(bottom),* IC–10
Eva Sakmar-Sullivan 21
Bill Thomson 2, 3 *(top),* 4, 5 *(bottom),* 8, 16 *(bottom),* 30 *(top),* 36, 37, 38, 49 *(bottom)*
Sam Viviano 10, 12 *(top),* 13, 15, 16 *(top),* 22 *(bottom),* 27, 33 *(top),* 34, 39, 42, 43, 44, 46, 51
Snapshots by Phil Scheuer

## Photographic Credits

The author and publisher are grateful for permission to reproduce the following photographs.

**3** *(center)* Reuters/Bettmann
**17** *(top)* © 1989 Jean Kugler/FPG International; *(bottom)* © Ken Ross/FPG International
**18** © 1993 Kenton/Zefa/H. Armstrong Roberts
**35** *(all)* © 1994 Erika Stone
**41** *(left to right)* © Daniel Bosler/Tony Stone Worldwide; courtesy United Airlines; K. Carpenter/H. Armstrong Roberts
**43** *(left to right)* E. Alan McGee/FPG International; SuperStock; © 1994 Erika Stone; SuperStock
**44** *(top)* J. B. Grant/Leo de Wys Inc.; *(bottom)* © J. Barry O'Rourke/The Stock Market
**47** *(left)* © 1993 Dick Luria/FPG International; *(middle and right)* © 1994 Erika Stone
**52** *(top)* © Daniel Bosler/Tony Stone Worldwide; *(middle)* Leo de Wys Inc., Leo de Wys; *(bottom)* © 1989 Chris Mihulka/The Stock Market
**53** *(top, left to right)* Camerique/H. Armstrong Roberts; M. Elenz-Tranter/H. Armstrong Roberts; SuperStock; © Keith Olson/Tony Stone Worldwide; *(bottom, left to right)* ©1987 Jon Feingersh/The Stock Market; © 1992 T. Tracy/FPG International; SuperStock
**IC–2** SuperStock
**IC–4** SuperStock
**IC–7** *Pyramids, Great Wall, and Taj Mahal:* SuperStock; *Acropolis:* Leo de Wys Inc./J. B. Grant

# Author's Acknowledgments

A great number of people assisted in writing *Interchange Intro*. Particular thanks go to the following:

The **students** and **teachers** in the following schools and institutes who pilot tested components of *Interchange Intro*; their valuable comments and suggestions helped shape the content of the entire course:

**Adult ESL Resource Centre,** Toronto, Canada; **The Bickford Centre,** Toronto, Canada; **Centro Cultural Salvadreño,** El Salvador; **Centro Internacional de Idiomas Maestros Asociados, S.C.,** Mexico; **Connections Language Consultants, Inc.,** Edmonton, Canada; **Dorset College,** Vancouver, Canada; **English Academy,** Japan; **Eurocentres,** Alexandria, Virginia, U.S.A.; **Fairmont State University,** West Virginia, U.S.A.; **Truman College,** Chicago, Illinois, U.S.A.; **Instituto Cultural de Idiomas Ltda,** Brazil; **Instituto Mexicano-Norteamericano de Cultura,** Mexico; **Language Resources,** Kobe, Japan; **Nippon Information and Communication Co.,** Japan; **Tokushima Bunri University,** Japan; and **University of California at Los Angeles Extension**, California, U.S.A.

And **editors** and **advisors** at Cambridge University Press, who provided guidance during the complex process of writing classroom materials:

Suzette André, Colin Bethell, Sarah Coleman, Riitta da Costa, Steve Dawson, Peter Donovan, Sandra Graham, Colin Hayes, John Haywood, Steven Maginn, Jane Mairs, Carine Mitchell, Noreen O'Connor-Abel, Susan Ryan, Helen Sandiford, Chuck Sandy, Ellen Shaw, Koen Van Landeghem, and Mary Vaughn.

# Introduction

*Interchange* is a multi-level course in English as a second or foreign language for young adults and adults. The course covers the skills of listening, speaking, reading, and writing, with particular emphasis on listening and speaking. The primary goal of the course is to teach communicative competence – that is, the ability to communicate in English according to the situation, purpose, and roles of the participants. *Interchange* reflects the fact that English is the world's major language of international communication and is not limited to any one country, region, or culture. The *Intro* level is designed for beginning students needing a thorough presentation of basic functions, grammar, and vocabulary. It prepares students to enter Level 1 of the course.

## COURSE LENGTH

*Interchange* is a self-contained course covering all four language skills. Each level covers between 60 and 90 hours of class instruction time. Depending on how the book is used, however, more or less time may be utilized. The Teacher's Manual gives detailed suggestions for optional activities to extend each unit. Where less time is available, a level can be taught in approximately 60 hours by reducing the amount of time spent on Interchange Activities, reading, writing, optional activities, and the Workbook.

## COURSE COMPONENTS OF INTRO

**Student's Book**   The Student's Book contains sixteen units, with a review unit after every four units. There are four review units in all. Following Unit 16 is a set of communicative activities called Interchange Activities, one for each unit of the book. Word lists at the end of the Student's Book contain key vocabulary and expressions used in each unit. The Student's Book is available in split edition, A and B, each containing 8 units.

**Teacher's Manual**   A separate Teacher's Manual contains detailed suggestions on how to teach the course, lesson-by-lesson notes, an extensive set of follow-up activities, complete answer keys to the Student's Book and Workbook exercises, four tests for use in class, test answer keys, and transcripts of those listening activities not printed in the Student's Book or in the tests. The tests can be photocopied

and distributed to students after each review unit is completed.

**Workbook**   The Workbook contains stimulating and varied exercises that provide additional practice on the teaching points presented in the Student's Book. A variety of exercise types is used to develop students' skills in grammar, reading, writing, spelling, vocabulary, and pronunciation. The Workbook can be used both for classwork and for homework. The Workbook is available in split editions.

**Class Cassettes**   A set of cassettes for class use accompanies the Student's Book. The cassettes contain recordings of the word power activities, conversations, grammar focus summaries, pronunciation exercises, listening activities, and readings, as well as recordings of the listening exercises used in the tests. A variety of native-speaker voices and accents is used, along with some non-native speakers of English. Exercises that are recorded on the cassettes are indicated with the symbol ▭.

**Student Cassettes**   Two cassettes are available for students to use for self-study. The Student Cassettes contain selected recordings of conversations, grammar, and pronunciation exercises from the Student's Book. Student Cassette A corresponds to Units 1–8 and Student Cassette B to Units 9–16.

## APPROACH AND METHODOLOGY

*Interchange* teaches students to use English for everyday situations and purposes related to work, school, social life, and leisure. The underlying philosophy of the course is that learning a second language is more rewarding, meaningful, and effective when the language is used for authentic communication. Information-sharing activities provide a maximum amount of student-generated communication. Throughout *Interchange,* students have the opportunity to personalize the language they learn and make use of their own life experiences and world knowledge.

The course has the following key features:

**Integrated Syllabus**   *Interchange* has an integrated, multi-skills syllabus that links grammar and communicative functions. The course recognizes grammar as an essential component of second language proficiency. However, it presents grammar communicatively, with controlled accuracy-based activities leading to fluency-based communicative practice. The syllabus also contains the four skills of listening, speaking, reading, and writing, as well as pronunciation and vocabulary.

**Adult and International Content**   *Interchange* deals with contemporary topics that are of high interest and relevance to both students and teachers. Each unit includes real-world information on a variety of topics.

**Enjoyable and Useful Learning Activities** A wide variety of interesting and enjoyable activities forms the basis for each unit. The course makes extensive use of pair work, small group activities, role plays, and information-sharing activities. Practice exercises allow for a maximum amount of individual student practice and enable learners to personalize and apply the language they learn. Throughout the course, natural and useful language is presented that can be used in real-life situations.

# WHAT EACH UNIT OF INTRO CONTAINS

Each unit in *Interchange* contains the following kinds of exercises:

**Snapshot**   The Snapshots provide interesting information about the world, introduce the topic of the unit and develop vocabulary. The teacher can either present these exercises in class as reading or discussion activities, or have students read them by themselves in class or for homework, using their dictionaries if necessary.

**Conversation**   The Conversations introduce the new grammar of each unit in a communicative context and present functions and conversational expressions. The teacher can either present the Conversations with the Class Cassettes or read the dialogs aloud.

**Pronunciation**   These exercises focus on important features of spoken English, including stress, rhythm, intonation, reductions, and sound contrasts.

**Grammar Focus**   The new grammar of each unit is presented in color panels and is followed by practice activities that move from controlled to freer practice. These activities always give students a chance to use the grammar they have learned for real communication.

**Listening**   The listening activities develop a wide variety of listening skills, including listening for gist, listening for details, and inferring meaning from context. These exercises often require completing an authentic task while listening, such as taking telephone messages. The recordings offer natural conversational English with the pauses, hesitations, and interruptions that occur in real speech.

**Word Power**   The Word Power activities develop students' vocabulary through a variety of interesting tasks, such as word maps. Most of these are recorded.

**Writing**   The writing exercises include practical writing tasks that extend and reinforce the teaching points in the unit and introduce students to composition skills. The Teacher's Manual shows how to use these exercises to focus on the process of writing.

**Reading**   Beginning in Unit 5, there are reading passages designed to develop a variety of reading skills, including guessing words from context, skimming, scanning, and making inferences. Various text types adapted from authentic sources are included.

**Interchange Activities**   The Interchange Activities are pair work and group work tasks involving information sharing and role playing to encourage real communication. These exercises are a central part of the course and allow students to extend and personalize what they have learned in each unit.

# 1 Hello. My name is Jennifer Wan.

## 1 SNAPSHOT

### POPULAR FIRST NAMES IN THE U.S.A.

| Females | | Males | |
|---|---|---|---|
| Jennifer | Sarah | Michael | John |
| Nicole | Deborah | Robert | Brian |
| Lisa | Mary | David | William |
| Michelle | Katherine | James | Steven |
| Linda | Jessica | Christopher | Matthew |

Complete the information.

My favorite girl's name in English: ........*Lisa*...............
My favorite boy's name in English: ........*William*..........
A popular first name in my country: ........*David,*...........

## 2 CONVERSATION 🔲

Listen and practice.

Jennifer: Hello. My name is Jennifer Wan.
Michael: Hi. I'm Michael Lynch.
Jennifer: Nice to meet you, Michael.
Michael: Nice to meet you, too, Jennifer.
        I'm sorry, what's your last name?
        Is it Wong?
Jennifer: No, *Wan*. W-A-N. And how do you
        spell Lynch?
Michael: L-Y-N-C-H.

## 3 THE ALPHABET 🔲

**1** Listen and practice.

A B C D E F G H I J K L M N O P Q R S T U V W X Y Z
a b c d e f g h i j k l m n o p q r s t u v w x y z

**2** *Pair work*  Spell your name. Then find out your partner's name
and your teacher's name. Spell their names.

2

# 4 GRAMMAR FOCUS: *my, your, his, her* 🔲

| | |
|---|---|
| What's **your** name? | **My** name is Jennifer. |
| What's **his** name? | **His** name is Michael. |
| What's **her** name? | **Her** name is Nicole. |

**What's = What is**

*Group work: "The Name Game"*   Make a circle.
Learn the names of your classmates.

A: My name is Juan.
B: His name is Juan. I'm Su Hee.
C: His name is Juan. Her name is Su Hee. I'm Keiko.

# 5 LISTENING 🔲

**1**   Who are they? Listen to the conversations. Spell their last names.

a) Whitney .....................
(She's a singer.)

b) Jackie ...........................
(He's a movie star.)

c) Steven ..... Spielberg
(He's a film director.)

**2**   *Pair work*   Cover the names. Now ask about each person.

A: What's her (his) name?
B: . . .
A: How do you spell her (his) name?
B: . . .

3

## 6 CONVERSATION

Listen and practice.

Victor:     Excuse me, are you Jennifer Wan?
Lisa:       No, I'm not. She's over there.
Victor:     I'm sorry.

Victor:     Excuse me, are you Jennifer Wan?
Jennifer:   Yes, I am.
Victor:     I think this is your book.
Jennifer:   You're right. It's my English book.
            Thank you.
Victor:     By the way, I'm Victor Garcia.
Jennifer:   It's nice to meet you, Victor.

## 7 GRAMMAR FOCUS: The verb *be*

| | | |
|---|---|---|
| **I'm** Victor Garcia. **You're** right. **She's** over there. (**Jennifer is** over there.) **He's** here. (**Victor is** here.) **It's** my English book. | **Are you** Jennifer Wan? **No, I'm not.** **Yes, I am.** | **I'm** = I am **You're** = You are **She's** = She is **He's** = He is **It's** = It is |

**1**  Complete the conversations.

Nicole: Excuse me, ...are... you Steven Carlson?
David:  No, ..I'm... not. ..He's.. over there. My name ...It's. David Bloom.
Nicole: Thanks, David.

Nicole: Are you Steven Carlson?
Steven: Yes, I ..am. .
Nicole: ..I'm. Nicole Johnson.
Steven: ...It's.nice to meet you. I think ..you're.in my math class.
Nicole: Yes, I ..am.. . And I think this ..is... your book.
Steven: Yes, ..It's. my math workbook. My name ..is.here. Thank you!

**2**  *Class activity*  Write your name on a piece of paper. Put it into a pile.
Choose the name of another student. Find the other student.

A: Excuse me, are you Maria Bravo?       A: Hi. Are you Maria Bravo?
B: No, I'm not.                          C: Yes, I am . . .

# 8 NUMBERS 🔊

**1** Listen and practice.

| 0 | 1 | 2 | 3 | 4 | 5 | 6 | 7 | 8 | 9 | 10 |
|---|---|---|---|---|---|---|---|---|---|---|
| zero (oh) | one | two | three | four | five | six | seven | eight | nine | ten |

**2** Say these numbers.

**3** *Group work* Make a list of the names and telephone numbers in your group.

A: What's your telephone number?
B: It's 555-2916.

# 9 LISTENING 🔊

Victor is making a list of telephone numbers of students in his class. He's talking to Sarah Smith. Listen and write the numbers.

| Name | Telephone number |
|---|---|
| David Bloom | |
| Steven Carlson | 555-9173 |
| Nicole Johnson | |
| Lisa Liu | |
| Michael Lynch | |
| Brian Noguchi | |
| Sarah Smith | |
| Jennifer Wan | 555-2947 |

▶ **Interchange 1: Directory Assistance**

Call Directory Assistance for some telephone numbers. Student A looks at page IC-2 and Student B looks at page IC-4.

## 🔟 WORD POWER 📼

**1** Listen, and complete with **a** or **an**.

a) This is ..... *a* .... book.

b) This is ..... *an* ..... English book.

c) This is ..... *a* .... notebook.

d) This is ..*an*.. eraser.

e) This is ..*a*.. dictionary.

f) This is *an*.... umbrella.

**2** Find these things in your classroom.

| | | |
|---|---|---|
| table *a* | map *a* | cassette player *a* |
| chair *a* | pencil *a* | wastebasket *a* |
| desk *a* | envelope *an* | English dictionary *an* |
| board *a* | piece of paper *a* | |

A: This is a table.
B: How do you spell *table*?
A: T-A-B-L-E.

## 1️⃣1️⃣ GREETINGS AND TITLES 📼

**1** Listen and practice. (**Mr., Mrs., Miss,** and **Ms.** are formal.)

*Saying hello*
Hi.
Hello.
Good morning.
Good afternoon.
Good evening.

*Saying good-bye*
Bye.
Bye-bye.
Good-bye. Have a nice day.
See you tomorrow.
Good night.

**2** Practice the expressions with your classmates.

# 12 INSTRUCTIONS 🔲

**1**  Listen.

a) Close your book, please.

b) Open your notebook.

c) Take out a pencil.

d) Write your name in your notebook.

e) Open your dictionary.

f) Find the word *eraser*.

g) Say the word *eraser*.

h) Please go to the board.

i) Write the word *eraser* on the board.

**2**  *Class activity*  Listen to your teacher. Follow the instructions.

**3**  *Pair work*  Write six instructions. Read the instructions to your partner. Then follow your partner's instructions.

# 2 What's this called in English?

## 1 SNAPSHOT

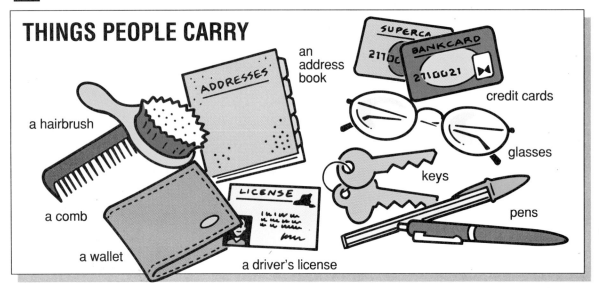

**THINGS PEOPLE CARRY**

- an address book
- credit cards
- a hairbrush
- glasses
- keys
- a comb
- pens
- a wallet
- a driver's license

What are you carrying today? .....................................................................................

## 2 SPELLING AND PRONUNCIATION: Plurals 🔲

Listen and practice. Notice the spelling.

| s = /s/ | | s = /z/ | | s = /ɪz/ | |
|---|---|---|---|---|---|
| book | book**s** | credit card | credit card**s** | glass | glass**es** |
| wallet | wallet**s** | key | key**s** | license | license**s** |
| map | map**s** | pen | pen**s** | hairbrush | hairbrush**es** |

## 3 CONVERSATION 🔲

Listen and practice.

Kumiko: What's this called in English, Sarah?
Sarah: It's an eyeglass case.
Kumiko: And what are these called? Eyeglasses?
Sarah: Eyeglasses, or just "glasses." And these are sunglasses.
Kumiko: Well, your sunglasses are very . . . nice.
Sarah: Thank you. They're new.

# 4 GRAMMAR FOCUS: *this, these*; singular and plural nouns ▭

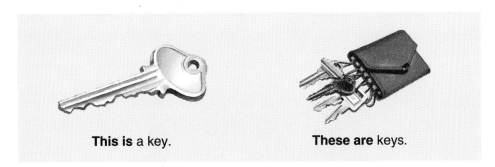

**This is** a key.          **These are** keys.

**1** What are these things called in English? Write a sentence for each item. Then listen to the sentences and practice them.

| handbag | tissues | photos | address book | umbrella |
|---------|---------|--------|--------------|----------|
| glasses | calculator | newspaper | briefcase | |

a) This is ...an umbrela... .    b) These are ...glasses... .    c) ...this is a calculator...

d) ...this is a handbag...  e) ...this is a briefcase...  f) ...this is a tissue...

g) ...this is a newspap...  h) ...this is a photo...  i) ...............

**2** *Pair work*  Put four things from your pocket, wallet, or bag on the desk. Cover them with a piece of paper. Your partner guesses what they are.

A: I think this is a credit card.
B: No.
A: It's a library card.
B: You're right.

## 5 CONVERSATION 🔲

Listen and practice.

| | |
|---|---|
| Mrs. Lee: | Excuse me, Katherine. Is this your umbrella? |
| Katherine: | Let me see. No, it's not. |
| Mrs. Lee: | Maybe it's Alice's umbrella. |
| Katherine: | No, her umbrella is different. Oh, I know. I think it's Daniel's. |
| Mrs. Lee: | Daniel, is this your umbrella? |
| Daniel: | Yes, it is. Thank you. Actually, it's my daughter's umbrella. |

## 6 GRAMMAR FOCUS: Possessives; yes/no questions with *be* 🔲

This is **my** umbrella.
This is **your** book.
This is **our** classroom.

These are **Robert's** keys. These are **his** keys.
These are **Sarah's** glasses. These are **her** glasses.

Mrs. Lee is **Katherine and Daniel's** teacher.
She is **their** teacher.

**Is this** Alice's umbrella?
Yes, **it is**.
No, **it's not**.

**Are these** Daniel's keys?
Yes, **they are**.
No, **they're not**.

Notice the pronunciation of the possessive **'s**:

| | |
|---|---|
| Robert**'s** | **/s/** |
| Daniel**'s** | **/z/** |
| Alice**'s** | **/ɪz/** |

**1** Complete the conversations. Then practice them.

A: ...*Is*... this your calculator?
B: No, it's ...*not*... . ...*My*... calculator is different.

A: ...*Are*... these Jennifer's sunglasses?
B: No, ...*they're*... not. Maybe they're Nicole's.

A: Mr. and Mrs. Lee, ...*Is*... your telephone number 555-1287?
B: No, ...*Our*... number is 555-2287.

A: ...*Is this*... Lisa's address book?
B: Yes, ...*it*... is. ...*Her*... name is right here.

A: ...*Are these*... your keys?
B: Yes, they ...*are*... . Thank you very much.

A: ...*Is this*... your newspaper?
B: Let me see. No, ...*it's not*... . It's Michael's. ...*His*... name and address are here.

**2** *Pair work*   Ask your partner a question about each picture.

A: Is this Yung's newspaper?
B: No, it's not his newspaper.

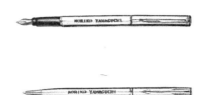

a) Yung                b) Noriko                c) Eric

d) Helen          e) Carmen and Hector          f) Julio

**3** *Group work*   Put three things from your wallet, briefcase, or handbag in a box. Find the owner of each item.

A: Is this your pen, Juan?
B: No, it's not. I think it's Su Hee's.

A: Is this your pen, Su Hee?
C: Let me see. Yes, it's my pen.

---

## 7  LISTENING 🔘

Sarah is cleaning up the classroom.
Who owns these things? Listen and check the right name.

|  | *Jennifer* | *Michael* | *Nicole* | *Steven* |
|---|---|---|---|---|
| calculator | ............. | calculator | ............. | ............. |
| sunglasses | ............. | ............. | sunglasses | ............. |
| book bag | ............. | ............. | ............. | book bag |
| hairbrush | hairbrush | ............. | ............. | ............. |

11

## 8 CONVERSATION 🔲

Listen and practice.

Mr. Brown: Thanks for watching the baby tonight. Everything is ready.
Katherine: Thank you, Mr. Brown. By the way, where is the television?
Mr. Brown: It's in this cabinet.
Katherine: And where is the remote control?
Mr. Brown: I don't know. Oh, it's on the sofa, under the cushion.
Katherine: Great. Oh, just one more question. Where is the baby?
Mr. Brown: She's in bed! Her bedroom is right there.

## 9 PREPOSITIONS OF PLACE 🔲

        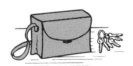       

| in | on | under | next to | behind | in front of |

Complete these sentences. Then listen to check your answers.

a) The briefcase is *in front of the television* .

b) The keys are *on the handbag* .

c) The wallet is *under the newspaper* .

d) The umbrella is *behind the wastebasket* .

e) The comb is *next to the hairbrush* .

f) The notebooks are *on the dictionary* .

# 10 LOST ITEMS

*Pair work*   You're late for work, and you need the things below.
Ask and answer the questions.

a) Where is my briefcase?   *is next to the chair*
b) Where is my address book?   *It's on the chair*
c) Where are my credit cards?   *they're under the table*
d) Where is my driver's license?   *It's on the table next to the newspaper*
e) Where is my pen?   *It's in the pocket*
f) Where are my glasses?   *they're in the briefcase*
g) Where is my umbrella?   *It's next to the chair*

▶ **Interchange 2:
Find the differences**
Look at two pictures of a room on
page IC-3 and find the differences.

# 11 INSTRUCTIONS 📼

**1**   Listen, and follow these instructions.

a) Pick up your book bag or your handbag.
b) Put it on your desk.
c) Take out your English book.
d) Put it next to your desk.
e) Take out your wallet.
f) Put it under your desk.
g) Take out a notebook.
h) Put it in front of your desk.

**2** *Pair work*   Give your partner instructions. Use **in**, **on**, **under**,
**next to**, **behind**, and **in front of**. Then follow your partner's instructions.

# 3 Where are you from?

## 1 SNAPSHOT

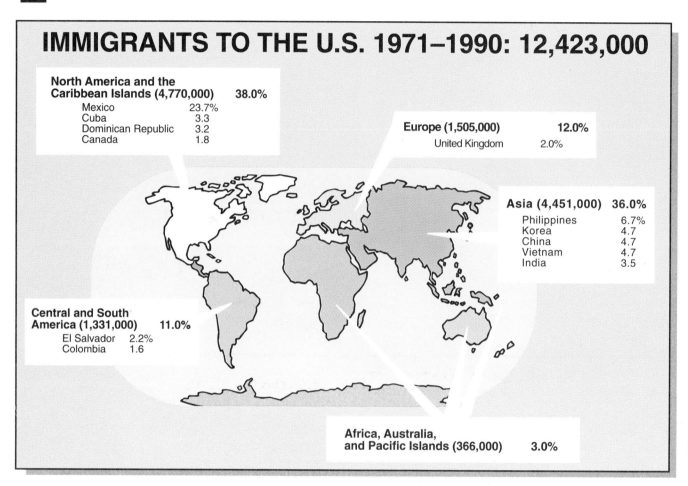

**IMMIGRANTS TO THE U.S. 1971–1990: 12,423,000**

**North America and the Caribbean Islands (4,770,000)** 38.0%

| | |
|---|---|
| Mexico | 23.7% |
| Cuba | 3.3 |
| Dominican Republic | 3.2 |
| Canada | 1.8 |

**Europe (1,505,000)** 12.0%

| | |
|---|---|
| United Kingdom | 2.0% |

**Asia (4,451,000)** 36.0%

| | |
|---|---|
| Philippines | 6.7% |
| Korea | 4.7 |
| China | 4.7 |
| Vietnam | 4.7 |
| India | 3.5 |

**Central and South America (1,331,000)** 11.0%

| | |
|---|---|
| El Salvador | 2.2% |
| Colombia | 1.6 |

**Africa, Australia, and Pacific Islands (366,000)** 3.0%

Are there immigrants in your country? *Yes There are*

Where are they from? *they are from germany, Italy, yapom, Potugal, Spain*

## 2 WORD POWER

*Class activity*  Name two more countries from each region.

*Europe*
*France, Spain, Potugal*

*Africa*
*Egypt, mauritania*

*Asia*
*china, Korea*

*North America and the Caribbean*
*Canada, cuba*

*Central and South America*
*México, El Salvador*

## 3 CONVERSATION 📼

**1** Listen and practice.

Mark: Where are you from, Laura?
Laura: Well, my whole family is in the United States now, but we're from Costa Rica originally.
Mark: Oh, so you're from South America.
Laura: Actually, Costa Rica isn't in South America. It's in Central America.
Mark: Oh, right. My geography isn't very good!

**2** Listen to the rest of the conversation.

a) Where is Mark from?
b) Where is his country?

## 4 GRAMMAR FOCUS: Statements with *be* 📼

| | | OR: |
|---|---|---|
| I'm | I'm not | |
| You're | You're not | You aren't |
| He's | He's not | He isn't |
| She's from Costa Rica. | She's not from El Salvador. | She isn't |
| It's | It's not | It isn't |
| We're | We're not | We aren't |
| They're | They're not | They aren't |

**1** *Pair work*  Complete the sentences as in the example. Compare answers with your partner.

a) Costa Rica is in Central America. *It's not* in South America.
b) My family is from Korea. We're in the U.S. now, but ............... from the U.S. originally.
c) Your glasses are on the table. ............... over there, next to the newspaper.
d) Hi, Sarah – oh, I'm sorry! ............... Sarah. Your name is Susan.
e) Where is my driver's license? ............... in my wallet! Where is it?
f) Katherine and I aren't in your class. ............... in Mrs. Lee's class.
g) Mr. Ho isn't from Hong Kong. ............... from Singapore.

15

**2**  Complete the conversations. Then practice them.

A: Where ............... Laura Sánchez from –
   South America?
B: No, she ............... from South America.
   ............... from Costa Rica.
A: Oh. So ............... from Central America.

A: Keiko, where ............... you and Kenji from?
B: ............... both from Japan.
A: Oh, ............... you from Tokyo?
B: No, we ............... from Tokyo.
   ............... from Kyoto.

A: Where ............... you from, Mr. **Park**?
B: ............... from the city of Pusan.
A: Where ............... Pusan, exactly?
   My geography ............... very good.
B: Pusan ............... in Korea.

---

**5**  **CONVERSATION** 🔲

Listen and practice.

Jack: Is this your newspaper?
Marta: Yes, it is. Here, take it.
Jack: Oh, but it isn't in English.
Marta: It's in Spanish. Spanish is my
   native language.
Jack: Really? Are you Spanish?
Marta: Actually, I'm not. I'm from
   Mexico.
Jack: Oh, so you're Mexican.
   That's interesting.

# 6 COUNTRIES AND NATIONALITIES 🔊

| Country | Nationality |
|---|---|
| They're from **Korea**. | They're **Korean**. |
| She's from **Mexico**. | She's **Mexican**. |

**1** Listen and practice. Notice the stressed syllables.

| | | | |
|---|---|---|---|
| **A**merica | A**mer**ican | **Spain** | **Span**ish |
| **Mex**ico | **Mex**ican | **Swe**den | **Swed**ish |
| Ko**re**a | Ko**re**an | **Ire**land | **Ir**ish |
| **Can**ada | Ca**na**dian | **Chi**na | Chi**nese** |
| **Hun**gary | Hun**gar**ian | **Por**tugal | **Por**tuguese |
| Bra**zil** | Bra**zil**ian | Ja**pan** | Japa**nese** |

**2** Listen and underline the stressed syllables.
Then practice the words.

| | | | |
|---|---|---|---|
| Colombia | Colombian | India | Indian |
| Egypt | Egyptian | Cambodia | Cambodian |
| England | English | Turkey | Turkish |
| Italy | Italian | Venezuela | Venezuelan |
| Poland | Polish | Vietnam | Vietnamese |
| Lebanon | Lebanese | Peru | Peruvian |

**3** *Pair work*  Complete the dialogues with the correct
country or nationality. Then practice them.

A: I'm from *Hungary*.
B: Oh, so you're Hungarian.

A: Is Mr. Lee from Korea?
B: No, he's *Chinese*.
He's from China.

A: Are you Vietnamese?
B: No, I'm not from *Vietnam*.
I'm from Cambodia.

A: Your newspaper is in Spanish.
B: Yes, it's a *Spanish* newspaper.
I'm from Mexico.

A: We're from Peru.
B: Oh, so you're *Peruvian*.
A: That's right.

A: Are you from *Japan* ?
B: Yes, we're Japanese.

**4** *Class activity*  Guess the country for each nationality.

| Country | Nationality | Country | Nationality |
|---|---|---|---|
| *Nepal* | Nepalese | *Cuba* | Cuban |
| *Bolivia* | Bolivian | *Sudan* | Sudanese |
| *Panama* | Panamanian | *New Zealand* | New Zealander |
| *Indonesia* | Indonesian | *France* | French |

17

# 7 | LANGUAGES 🔊

**THE TOP 10
LANGUAGES
OF THE WORLD**

1. Chinese
2. English
3. Hindi
4. Spanish
5. Russian
6. Arabic
7. Bengali
8. Portuguese
9. Japanese
10. German

**THE 6 OFFICIAL
LANGUAGES
OF THE
UNITED NATIONS**

1. Arabic
2. Chinese
3. English
4. French
5. Russian
6. Spanish

What is your native language? *It's Portuguese*
What is the official language of your
country? *official language Portuguese*

**1** *Class activity* What are the official languages of these countries?
What is another country with the same language?

A: German is the language of Austria.
B: German is the language of Germany, too.

a) Austria ....... *It's german* .......
b) Brazil ....... *It's portuguese* .......
c) Chile ....... *It's Spanish* .......

d) Morocco ....... *It's Arabic* .......
e) New Zealand ....... *It's English* .......

**2** *Pair work* What do you think these languages are?

A: I think this is Spanish.
B: Yes, it's Spanish.

a)
Yo soy un hombre sincero
De donde crece la palma,
Y antes de morirme quiero
Echar mis versos del alma.

b)
Longtemps, je me suis
couché de bonne heure.
Parfois, à peine ma bougie
éteinte, mes yeux se
fermaient si vite que je
n'avais pas le temps de
me dire : « Je m'endors. »

c)
原因は味?安全?

d)
夜思
牀前明月光。
疑是地上霜。
舉頭望明月，
低頭思故鄉。

e)
Очень просто. По окончани
Казанского авиационного институт
ждала распределения. Могли направи
инженером на завод или младшим нау
ным сотрудником в НИИ – бумажки г

f)
Eine Revolution raschelt durch die Republik:
Jährlich drei Milliarden Fax-Seiten decken
Privathaushalte und Unternehmen ein.

g)
Para além do seu valor clínic
medicamentos modernos
proporcionam muitas vezes un
eficácia de valor acrescentado
para os cuidados de saúde.

## 8 LISTENING 🔲

Antonio, Mei-Ling, and Monique meet for the first time. Where are they from?
What are their native languages?

| | Country | Nationality | Language |
|---|---|---|---|
| a) Antonio | *Brasil* | *Brazilian* | *Portuguese* |
| b) Mei-Ling | *China* | *Chinese* | *Chinese* |
| c) Monique | *Canada* | *Canadian* | *French* |

## 9 GRAMMAR FOCUS: Questions and short answers with *be* 🔲

**Are** you from Canada?
   **Yes, I am.**
   **No, I'm not.**

**Is** Mary from New Zealand?
   **Yes, she is.**
   **No, she's not. (No, she isn't.)**

**Is** this handbag from Korea?
   **Yes, it is.**
   **No, it's not. (No, it isn't.)**

**Are** you and Lisa Chinese?
   **Yes, we are.**
   **No, we're not. (No, we aren't.)**

**Are** they from Japan?
   **Yes, they are.**
   **No, they're not. (No, they aren't.)**

**1** Match the questions and the answers. Then practice with a partner.

a) Is your first name Jennifer? *3*

b) Are you Michael Lynch? *6*

c) Is English your native language? *4*

d) Are these your keys? *1*

e) Are you and your family from the United States? *2*

f) Are your credit cards in your wallet? *5*

1) No, they're not. My keys are different.
2) Yes, we are. We're from San Francisco.
3) Yes, it is. And my last name is Wan.
4) No, it's not. It's Japanese.
5) Yes, they are. They're in my wallet next to my driver's license.
6) No, I'm not. I'm David Bloom.

▶ **Interchange 3: Geography quiz**
Turn to pages IC-6 and IC-7 for a quiz on monuments in Europe, Africa, and Asia.

**2** *Pair work* Write five questions to ask your partner. Then take turns asking questions.

# 4 Clothes and weather

## 1 SNAPSHOT

**CLOTHES FROM AROUND THE WORLD**

**Wristwatches** are originally from France. (1907)

**Blue jeans** are originally from the United States. (1850s)

**Bathing suits** are originally from England. (19th century)

**Neckties** are originally from Croatia. (17th century)

**High heels** are originally from France. (17th century)

**Pajamas** are originally from India. (date unknown)

What clothes are originally from your country? ...... *Shorts* ...... *skirt, Shoes hat Shirt.*

---

## 2 COLORS

**1** Listen and practice.

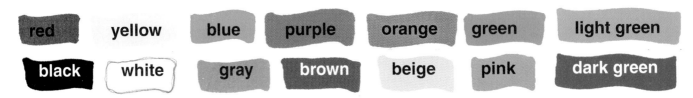

red   yellow   blue   purple   orange   green   light green

black   white   gray   brown   beige   pink   dark green

**2** *Pair work* Ask about colors.

A: What are your favorite colors? *My favorite color are: red, blue green*

B: My favorite colors are green and purple.

20

# 3 WORD POWER: Clothes 🔊

**1**  What color are these things? Listen and practice.

*The suit is gray. The blouse is white . . .*

suit *gray*    blouse *white*    skirt *green*    dress *pink*

slacks *brown*    shirt *blue*    tie *orange*    coat *beige*

shorts *white*    running shoes *purple*    hat *gray*    boots *dark green*

scarf *yellow*    T-shirt *red*    shoes *gray*

**2**  *Pair work*  Ask and answer questions about the clothes.

A: What color is the suit?
B: It's gray.

A: What color are the slacks?
B: They're light brown.

21

**3** *Pair work* Fill in the chart with words from pages 20 and 21.
Add two more words to each list.

| Clothes for warm weather | Clothes for cold weather |
|---|---|
| | |

## 4 CONVERSATION 🔲

Listen and practice.

Susan: Uh-oh.
Peter: What's the matter?
Susan: It's snowing, and it's very cold.
Peter: Well, you're wearing a coat.
Susan: But I'm not wearing boots!
And it's thirty-two degrees.
Peter: That's zero degrees Celsius!
That's really cold.
Susan: So let's take a taxi.
Peter: Great idea. Come on!

# 5 GRAMMAR FOCUS: Present continuous; *and, but, so* ▭

| I'm | I'm not | |
|---|---|---|
| You're | you aren't | |
| She's | wearing a coat, but she isn't | wearing boots. |
| We're | we aren't | |
| They're | they aren't | |

It's snowing, **and** it's very cold.

I'm wearing a coat, **but** I'm not wearing boots.

It's very cold, **so** let's take a taxi.

**1** Complete these sentences with the information below. Then listen and practice.

a) She's running, so . . .

b) He's driving, but . . .

c) We're walking in the snow, but . . .

d) She's swimming, and . . .

e) They're playing tennis, but . . .

f) It's snowing, and . . .

1) . . . I'm taking a walk.
2) . . . we aren't wearing boots.
3) . . . she's wearing running shoes.
4) . . . they aren't wearing tennis shoes.
5) . . . she's wearing a green bathing suit.
6) . . . he isn't wearing his glasses.

| Notice the spelling of the continuous verb form: | | |
|---|---|---|
| wear | = | **wearing** |
| swim | = | **swimming** (+ m) |
| drive | = | **driving** (− e) |

23

**2** *Pair work*   Complete the sentences about each picture. Compare answers with a partner.

a) We ...*'re wearing*........... bathing suits, but
   we ...*aren't swimming*..... .
   (wear, swim)

b) He ................................. , and
   she ................................. .
   (drive, run)

c) It ............................... , and
   they ............................... .
   (snow, swim)

d) They ............................... basketball, so
   they ............................... shorts.
   (play, wear)

e) He ............................... today, so
   he ............................... a suit and tie.
   (work, wear)

f) She ............................... a briefcase, but
   she ............................... a handbag.
   (carry, carry)

**3** *Class activity*   Write three true sentences and three false
sentences about your classmates. Then read them to the class.
Your classmates say "right" or "wrong."

A: Su Hee is wearing black shoes.
B: That's right.

A: Juan is wearing a suit and tie.
B: That's wrong. He's wearing a suit,
   but he isn't wearing a tie.

# 6 NUMBERS 📼

Listen and practice.

| | | | | | |
|---|---|---|---|---|---|
| 11 | eleven | 21 | twenty-one | 40 | forty |
| 12 | twelve | 22 | twenty-two | 50 | fifty |
| 13 | thirteen | 23 | twenty-three | 60 | sixty |
| 14 | fourteen | 24 | twenty-four | 70 | seventy |
| 15 | fifteen | 25 | twenty-five | 80 | eighty |
| 16 | sixteen | 26 | twenty-six | 90 | ninety |
| 17 | seventeen | 27 | twenty-seven | 100 | one hundred |
| 18 | eighteen | 28 | twenty-eight | 101 | one hundred and one |
| 19 | nineteen | 29 | twenty-nine | 102 | one hundred and two |
| 20 | twenty | 30 | thirty | | |

# 7 TEMPERATURES

**1** Match the Fahrenheit and equivalent Celsius temperatures. Practice with a partner.

A: What is ............ degrees Fahrenheit?    B: It's ............ degrees Celsius.

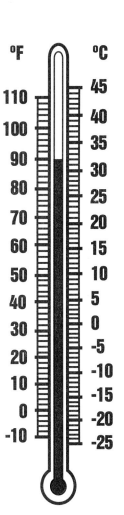

a) ninety
b) one hundred and four
c) seventy-two
d) three
e) fifty
f) eighty-six
g) sixty-six

............ nineteen
............ twenty-two
............ ten
............ thirty
............ thirty-two
............ forty
............ sixteen below zero

**2** *Pair work*   Ask and answer questions.

A: What is the temperature in ................... ?
B: It's ............ Celsius. (It's ............ Fahrenheit.)

## Temperatures around the world for February 1

| city | temperature F | C | city | temperature F | C |
|---|---|---|---|---|---|
| Buenos Aires | 82 | 28 | São Paulo | 89 | 32 |
| Moscow | 12 | -11 | Sydney | 85 | 29 |
| Paris | 46 | 8 | Taipei | 64 | 18 |
| Quebec City | 3 | -16 | Tokyo | 43 | 6 |
| San Francisco | 60 | 15 | Vancouver | 41 | 5 |

# 8 WHAT'S THE WEATHER LIKE? 📼

Listen and practice.

It's spring.
It's raining. It's cool.
It's fifty degrees.

It's summer.
It's warm and sunny.
It's eighty.

It's summer.
It's very hot and humid.
It's ninety-five.

It's fall.
It's windy.
It's cool. It's cloudy.

It's winter.
It's very cold.
It's five degrees.

It's winter.
It's snowing.
It's thirty-two degrees.

# 9 LISTENING 📼

Listen to the weather reports for the cities below. Write the temperature
and check off the weather conditions.

| | Temperature | hot | warm | cool | cold | sunny | cloudy | raining | snowing |
|---|---|---|---|---|---|---|---|---|---|
| | | | | | | *Conditions* | | | |
| a) Sapporo (Japan) | .......... | ☐ | ☐ | ☐ | ☐ | ☐ | ☐ | ☐ | ☐ |
| b) Bangkok (Thailand) | .......... | ☐ | ☐ | ☐ | ☐ | ☐ | ☐ | ☐ | ☐ |
| c) Miami (U.S.A.) | .......... | ☐ | ☐ | ☐ | ☐ | ☐ | ☐ | ☐ | ☐ |
| d) Rio de Janeiro (Brazil) | .......... | ☐ | ☐ | ☐ | ☐ | ☐ | ☐ | ☐ | ☐ |

# 10 CLOTHES AND WEATHER

**1** *Pair work* What's the weather like in these pictures?
What are the people wearing? Write three sentences about each picture.
Then compare sentences with your partner.

> a) It's cold. It's 28 degrees. She's wearing . . .

**a**

**b**

**c**

**2** *Pair work* Ask and answer these questions.

What's the weather like today in your city?
What are you wearing today?

▶ **Interchange 4: What's the weather like?**

What's the weather like in North and South America on February 1? Look at the map on page IC-5.

# Review of Units 1–4

## 1 Prepositions of place

*Group work*   Identify two items from your bag, briefcase, or wallet.
Give them to your classmates. Your classmates put the items in a different
place. Ask where the items are.

A:  This is my driver's license.
B:  These are my keys . . .

A:  Where is my driver's license?
B:  It's under your chair . . .

## 2 Listening 🔊

Tim is looking for things in his room. His mother is
helping him. Listen and mark the location of each item
in the picture.

a)

b)

c)

d)

e)

## 3 Same or different?

*Pair work*   Choose two classmates. Are their clothes the same or different?
Write five sentences and then compare with a partner.

| Same | Different |
| --- | --- |
| Juan and Victor are both | Juan is wearing boots, |
| wearing blue jeans. | but Victor is wearing shoes. |

28

# 4 │ Instructions

*Pair work* Complete the instructions below. Read the instructions to your partner. Follow your partner's instructions.

a) Close ............................................
b) Open ............................................
c) Take out ............................................
d) Say ............................................
e) Go ............................................

f) Write ............................................
g) Spell ............................................
h) Pick up ............................................
i) Put ............................................
j) Carry ............................................

# 5 │ What's the question?

**1** Match the questions and the answers. Then practice with a partner.

a) What's your name? ..............
b) What's this called in English? ..............
c) How do you spell *calculator*? ..............
d) Where is my English book? ..............
e) Where are you from? ..............
f) What color are your shoes? ..............
g) What's the weather like today? ..............
h) What's the temperature today? ..............
i) What is your teacher wearing today? ..............
j) What's your telephone number? ..............

1) It's C-A-L-C-U-L-A-T-O-R.
2) It's 555-3493.
3) It's windy and it's raining.
4) It's eighty-five degrees Fahrenheit.
5) We're from Thailand.
6) It's Sarah Smith.
7) He's wearing a suit and tie.
8) It's a driver's license.
9) It's under your chair.
10) They're black.

**2** *Pair work* Ask and answer the same questions. Answer with personal information.

# 6 │ What's strange about this picture?

*Pair work* Find five strange things in the picture. Write a sentence about each one. Compare your sentences with a partner.

> A woman is swimming, and she's wearing a blouse and a hat.

# 5 What are you doing?

## 1 CONVERSATION 🔊

Listen and practice.

Deborah: Hello?
John: Hi, Deborah! This is John. I'm calling from Australia.
Deborah: What are you doing in Australia?
John: I'm attending a conference in Sydney this week. Remember?
Deborah: Oh, right. What time is it there?
John: It's 10:00 P.M. And it's four o'clock in Los Angeles, right?
Deborah: Yes – four o'clock in the morning.
John: 4:00 A.M? I'm really sorry.
Deborah: That's OK. I'm awake now.

## 2 WHAT TIME IS IT? (1) 🔊

**1** Listen and practice.

What time is it?
It's five o'clock in the morning.
It's 5:00 A.M.

It's seven o'clock in the morning.
It's 7:00 A.M.

It's twelve o'clock.
It's noon.
(It's 12:00 noon.)

It's four o'clock in the afternoon.
It's 4:00 P.M.

It's seven o'clock in the evening.
It's 7:00 P.M.

It's twelve o'clock at night.
It's midnight.
(It's 12:00 midnight.)

**2** Say it another way.

a) It's eight o'clock in the evening. *It's 8:00 P.M.*
b) It's twelve o'clock at night.
c) It's three o'clock in the afternoon.

d) It's 3:00 A.M.
e) It's 9:00 A.M.
f) It's 4:00 P.M.

# 3 GRAMMAR FOCUS: Present continuous: *What + doing* 🔲

**1** Listen and practice.

What is Victoria doing?
She's sleeping.

What is Juan doing?
He's getting up.

What are Sue and Tom doing?
They're having breakfast.

What is Celia doing?
She's going to work.

What are Paul and Ann doing?
They're having lunch.

What is Boris doing?
He's working.

What is Permsak doing?
He's having dinner.

What is Jim doing?
He's watching television.

What are you doing?
I'm . . .

**2** *Pair work*   Ask and answer questions about the pictures.

a) What time is it in Los Angeles?
b) What is Victoria doing?
c) Where are Sue and Tom?
d) What are they doing?

e) Who is working right now?
f) What is Juan wearing?
g) What is he doing?
h) Who is carrying a briefcase?

## 4 LISTENING 📼

It's 7:00 P.M. in New York. Sue and Tom are calling their friends in different cities. What time is it in Bangkok? Tokyo? Brasília?

▶**Interchange 5: Time zones**

Talk about what people are doing in different cities of the world. Turn to page IC-8.

## 5 SNAPSHOT

**TELLING TIME**

alarm clock    clock radio    watch    digital watch    sports watch

How many watches or clocks do you own? .......................................................
What kind are they? ...................................................................................

## 6 WHAT TIME IS IT? (2) 📼

**1**   Listen and practice.

It's five minutes after three.        It's ten minutes after five.        It's 9:30 (nine thirty).
It's 3:05 (three-oh-five).            It's 5:10 (five-ten).

It's a quarter to eleven.        It's a quarter after seven.        It's twenty-five to eleven.
It's 10:45.                      It's 7:15.                          It's 10:35.

**2**   *Pair work*   Look at these clocks. What time is it?

A: What time is it?
B: It's twenty minutes after two. (It's 2:20.)

# 7 CONVERSATION

Listen and practice.

Mr. Ford:   Hey! Are you getting dressed?
Mrs. Ford:  Yes, I am.
Mr. Ford:   Why? What time is it?
Mrs. Ford:  It's a quarter to eight. I'm going to work.
Mr. Ford:   But it's Saturday.
Mrs. Ford:  I'm working on Saturday mornings this month. Are you getting up?
Mr. Ford:   No, I'm not. I'm staying in bed.
Mrs. Ford:  OK. See you at noon.
Mr. Ford:   If I'm awake.

# 8 PRONUNCIATION

**1** Listen to the intonation of statements and yes/no questions.

I'm getting up now.      Are you getting up?

He's having breakfast.    Is she having breakfast?

**2** Now listen to these sentences. Are they yes/no questions or statements? Circle **Q** or **S**.

a) Q  S     c) Q  S     e) Q  S

b) Q  S     d) Q  S     f) Q  S

# 9 LISTENING: Saturday chores

Listen to the sounds of some Saturday chores. Number the pictures from 1 to 4.

a) ........       b) ........       c) ........       d) ........

*vacuuming*      *washing the dishes*      *shopping*      *cleaning the house*

# 10 GRAMMAR FOCUS: Present continuous: yes/no questions 🔳

| Are you getting up? | Is he having breakfast? | Is she going to work? | Are they working? |
|---|---|---|---|
| Yes, I am. | Yes, he is. | Yes, she is. | Yes, they are. |
| No, I'm not. | No, he isn't. | No, she isn't. | No, they aren't. |

**1** *Pair work*    Ask and answer questions about the Fords. Use the verbs.

A: What time is it?
B: It's a quarter to eight.
A: Is Mrs. Ford getting dressed?
B: Yes, she is.
A: Is Mr. Ford getting dressed?
B: No, he isn't. He's sleeping.

get dressed?

work?

clean the house?

shop?

go to the movies?

dance?

**2** *Pair work*    Write five more questions about the Fords.
Then ask and answer the questions with a partner.

It's 2:15. Is Mr. Ford sleeping? . . .

# 11 **READING** 🔲

**1** Find the picture for each paragraph.

## It's Saturday!
## What are you doing today?

a) .........      b) .........      c) .........      d) .........

CHRIS JOHNSON: What am I doing? I'm shopping for summer clothes. This bathing suit is great. I'm also looking for sandals. I'm getting ready for a vacation at the beach.

TERRY RIVERA: We're working in the garden today. We're planting flowers and pulling weeds. This is our favorite thing to do on a Saturday.

STACY CHEN: My friend and I are just driving around and looking at people. We're not doing anything special. But we're having fun.

PAT EDWARDS: I'm just sitting outdoors, in a café. And I'm having coffee, of course. I'm reading a great book. It's a love story. Uh-oh. It's starting to rain.

**2** Add these sentences to the paragraphs.

a) But we're feeling tired now.
b) And I'm not carrying an umbrella.
c) I'm looking for sunglasses, too.
d) We're listening to music on the car radio.

**3** *Group work* Imagine you and your classmates are together on a Saturday. Write five sentences about what you are doing.

> *We're listening to the radio . . .*

# 6 How do you go to work?

## 1 SNAPSHOT

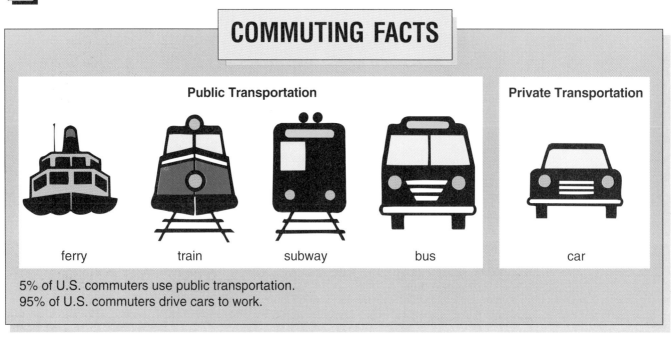

**COMMUTING FACTS**

**Public Transportation**

ferry     train     subway     bus

**Private Transportation**

car

5% of U.S. commuters use public transportation.
95% of U.S. commuters drive cars to work.

How do people go to work or school in your city? ..............................................
How do you go to work or school? ..............................................

## 2 CONVERSATION 🖾

Listen and practice.

Julia: Hi, Charles. What's the matter?
Charles: My car isn't working. I'm waiting for a tow truck.
Julia: Do you have a ride home?
Charles: Yes, my wife is coming to get me.
Julia: That's good. Do you live near here?
Charles: No, we live in the suburbs. What about you?
Julia: I live downtown, with my parents.
Charles: Do you have a car?
Julia: I don't need a car. I walk to work.
Charles: You're lucky!

# 3 WORD POWER: Family relationships 📼

Complete the sentences about the picture.
Then listen to check your answers.

a) Anne is Charles's ..*wife*.......... .
b) Jason and Sophia are his ..................... .
c) Charles is Anne's ..................... .
d) Jason is Anne's ..................... .
e) Sophia is Anne's ..................... .
f) Jason is Sophia's ..................... .
g) Sophia is Jason's ..................... .
h) Charles and Anne are
   Jason's ..................... .

# 4 LISTENING 📼

**1** Listen to Charles talk about his family. Practice the sentences.

My wife and I live in the suburbs.
We drive to work, but we don't
   drive together.
We have two cars.
Our children go to school by bus.

My parents live in the country.
My father drives to work.
My mother doesn't work
   because she's retired now.

My sister has an apartment
   in the city.
She lives alone.
She walks to work.
She doesn't have a car.

**2** *Pair work*    Listen to people in Charles's family talking. Who are they?

a) .........    1) his wife, Anne
b) .........    2) his mother
c) .........    3) his daughter, Sophia
d) .........    4) his sister

# 5 GRAMMAR FOCUS: Present tense statements

**Regular verbs**

| I | **live** |
|---|---|
| You | **live** |
| He/She | **lives** in the suburbs. |
| We | **live** |
| They | **live** |

| I | **don't live** |
|---|---|
| You | **don't live** |
| He/She | **doesn't live** in the city. |
| We | **don't live** |
| They | **don't live** |

**Irregular verbs**

I **have** a car.
My wife **has** a car, too.
We both **go** to work by car.
My son **goes** to school by bus.
I **do** my work in an office.
My son **does** his work at school.

**1** Complete Julia's sentences with the correct verb form. Then listen to check your answers.

a) I ............... (live, lives) with my parents.
b) We ............... (live, lives) downtown.
c) My parents ............... (has, have) an apartment.
d) I ............... (walk, walks) to work.
e) I ............... (don't, doesn't) need a car.
f) My mother ............... (don't, doesn't) walk to work.
g) She ............... (use, uses) public transportation.
h) She ............... (take, takes) the subway.
i) My father is retired, so he ............... (don't, doesn't) have a job.
j) But he ............... (do, does) a lot of work at home.
k) He also ............... (watch, watches) television.
l) I ............... (has, have) a brother and a sister.
m) My sister ............... (has, have) a husband and three children.
n) They ............... (live, lives) in a house in the country.
o) The children ............... (go, goes) to school by bus.
p) My brother ............... (has, have) an apartment in the city.
q) He ............... (live, lives) alone.
r) He ............... (don't, doesn't) have a car.
s) He ............... (use, uses) public transportation.
t) He ............... (go, goes) to work by bus.

**2** *Pair work* Write five sentences about you and your family. Use the sentences above as a model. Then compare with a partner.

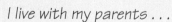
*I live with my parents . . .*

**3** *Class activity* Are you and your partner the same or different? Tell the class.

"I live with my parents, but Keiko lives alone. We both drive to class . . ."

# 9 DAYS OF THE WEEK 🔊

**1**   Listen and practice.

| Sunday | Monday | Tuesday | Wednesday | Thursday | Friday | Saturday |
|---|---|---|---|---|---|---|

**2** *Pair work*   Ask and answer questions.

a) What do you do on Saturdays? On Sundays? On Mondays?
b) What time do you go to bed on weekdays? On the weekend?
c) Do you have a job? What days do you work?
d) What days do you have English class?
e) What is your favorite day of the week? Why?

| Weekdays | Weekend |
|---|---|
| Monday | Saturday |
| Tuesday | and |
| Wednesday | Sunday |
| Thursday | |
| Friday | |

# 10 READING 🔊

**1**   One piece of information (one word) in each paragraph is incorrect.
Can you find it? Listen to check your answers.

## What's your work schedule?

**Randall Kelly   Restaurant cook**

"I get up at 5:00 A.M., get dressed, and drive to work. The restaurant opens at 6:00 A.M. sharp. We serve breakfast until eleven and lunch until three. Then I go home. I go to bed at around nine, and hope that the telephone doesn't ring. Luckily, I don't work on Saturdays or Sundays, I only work on weekends."

**Andrea Morris  Flight attendant**

"Sometimes I go to work at 5:00 A.M., and sometimes I go at 5:00 P.M. Sometimes I leave the house on Monday and don't come home until Wednesday. I often work on weekends. My job is interesting, but my schedule is regular. And I don't see my husband enough."

**Rob Jefferson       Rock musician**

"I go to work at ten o'clock in the evening, and I play until 3:00 A.M. I take a break at midnight, though. After work I have dinner at an all-night restaurant. Then I take a taxi home. I go to bed at five in the morning and sleep until two in the morning. I only work three nights a week – Friday, Saturday, and Sunday."

**2**   Answer the questions.

a) Who gets up early? Who gets up late?
b) Who works at night? Who works during the day?
c) Who works on weekends? Who works on weekdays?
d) Find one thing you like about each person's schedule.

**3**   Write five sentences about your schedule.

# 7 Does the apartment have a view?

## 1 SNAPSHOT

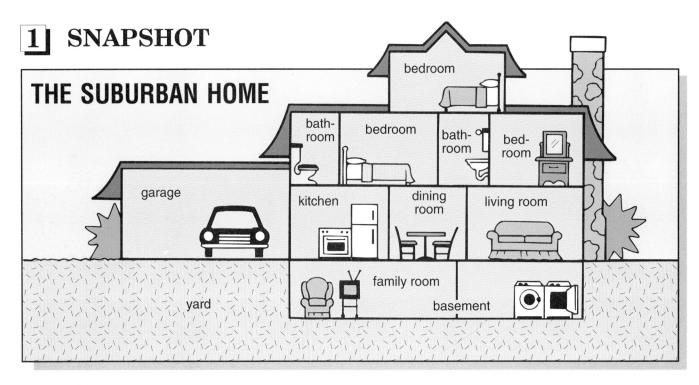

THE SUBURBAN HOME

bedroom

bath-room · bedroom · bath-room · bed-room

garage · kitchen · dining room · living room

family room · basement

yard

What rooms do houses have in your country? ..........................................
What rooms do apartments have in your country? ..........................................

## 2 CONVERSATION 📼

Listen and practice.

Linda: Guess what! I have a new apartment.
      I'm moving in this weekend.
Chris: Really? Do you need help?
Linda: Well, yes, I do. Thank you!
Chris: No problem.

Chris: So what is the apartment like?
      How many rooms does it have?
Linda: Well, it has a bedroom, a kitchen,
      and a living room. And a big closet.
Chris: That's great. Where is it?
Linda: It's on Lakeview Drive.
Chris: Oh. Does it have a view?
Linda: Yes, it does. It has a great view
      of my neighbor's apartment!

## **3** **GRAMMAR FOCUS:** Present tense questions and short answers 🔲

**Do** you **live** in an apartment?
  Yes, I **do**.
  No, I **don't**.

**Does** the apartment **have** a view?
  Yes, it **does**.
  No, it **doesn't**.

**Do** the bedrooms **have** closets?
  Yes, they **do**.
  No, they **don't**.

How many rooms **does** the apartment **have**?
  It **has** four rooms.

**1**  Complete the conversation with verbs. Then practice with a partner.

Linda: ................ you ................ in an apartment?
Chris: No, I ................ . I ................ in a house.
Linda: What is it like? ................ it ................ a yard?
Chris: Yes, it ................ . And it's next to the river.
Linda: That sounds great. ................ you ................ alone?
Chris: No, I ................ . I ................ with my parents and my sisters.
Linda: How many sisters ................ you ................ ?
Chris: I ................ four.
Linda: That's a big family. ................ you ................ a big house?
Chris: Yes, we ................ . It ................ ten rooms.
Linda: Ten rooms! How many bedrooms ................ it ................ ?
Chris: It ................ four.
Linda: ................ you ................ your own bedroom?
Chris: Yes, I ................ . I'm really lucky.
Linda: ................ your bedroom ................ a view of the river?
Chris: No, it ................ . It's in the basement.

**2**  *Pair work*   Write five questions to ask your partner about his or her house or apartment. Then ask your questions.

> *Do you live in an apartment? . . .*

## **4** **LISTENING** 🔲

Listen to people describe their house or apartment. Number the pictures from 1 to 4.

a) ............     b) ............     c) ............     d) ............

# 5 DREAM HOUSE

**1** Write a description of your dream house.

Where is your dream house?
How many rooms does it have?
What are the rooms?
What else does it have?

> *My dream house is in the country.*
> *It has twenty rooms . . .*

**2** *Pair work* Ask your partner about his or her dream house.

A: Does it have a swimming pool?
B: Yes, it does.

# 6 CONVERSATION 🔲

Listen and practice.

Chris: This apartment is very nice.
Linda: Yes, but I need some furniture.
Chris: What do you need?
Linda: Well, there's a table in the kitchen, but there aren't any chairs.
Chris: And there's no sofa in the living room.
Linda: Right. There are only two armchairs.
Chris: So, let's go to a yard sale next weekend.
Linda: That's a great idea!

# 7 WORD POWER

**1**   You need furniture for your apartment. Choose things at the yard sale.
Make a list for each room.

| *kitchen* | *dining room* | *living room* | *bedroom* |
|---|---|---|---|
| .................... | .................... | .................... | .................... |
| .................... | .................... | .................... | .................... |
| .................... | .................... | .................... | .................... |
| .................... | .................... | .................... | .................... |
| .................... | .................... | .................... | .................... |
| .................... | .................... | .................... | .................... |

**2**   Add three more things to each list.

**3**   *Pair work*   Compare lists with your partner. What do you need?

"For the kitchen, I need a stove, a refrigerator, and . . ."

# 8 GRAMMAR FOCUS: *there is/there are* 🔲

**There's a** table in the kitchen.
**There's no** sofa in the living room.
**There are some** armchairs in the living room.
**There aren't any** chairs in the kitchen.

**There's = There is**

**1** *Pair work*   Say what furniture Linda has in each room.
Your partner says what furniture is missing.

A: There's a mirror in the bedroom.
B: There's no dresser in the bedroom.

**2** *Pair work*   Write five sentences about things
you have or don't have in your classroom.
Compare sentences with your partner.

*There are twenty desks in the room.*
*There aren't any pictures on the wall . . .*

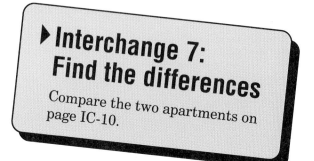

▶**Interchange 7:**
**Find the differences**
Compare the two apartments on
page IC-10.

## 9 PRONUNCIATION: /ð/ and /θ/ 📼

**1** Listen and practice.

/ð/     /θ/          /ð/       /ð/         /θ/     /θ/

**Th**ere are **th**irteen rooms in **th**e house. **Th**e house has **th**ree ba**th**rooms.

**2** Find three more words with /ð/ and three more words with /θ/.

| /ð/ | /θ/ |
|-----|-----|
| ..................................... | ..................................... |
| ..................................... | ..................................... |
| ..................................... | ..................................... |

## 10 READING 📼

# What's your favorite room?

**Joseph Landi:**

My favorite room is the kitchen. We have a big kitchen, with a modern stove and refrigerator. There's a big dining table, so we always eat dinner here together. I cook every evening and weekend. My children cook, too, but they only use the microwave oven.

**Liz Johnson:**

My favorite room is my bedroom. It's my "private study." I have a desk, a bookcase, and a computer in here. I also have a bed, of course. It's the room where I read, study, play computer games, and sleep.

**Susan Stern:**

The living room is my favorite room. It's the room where I relax at night. There are some beautiful pictures on the wall. There's a comfortable sofa. I sit on the sofa and watch TV every evening. Sometimes I listen to music on the stereo system.

**1** Complete the chart. What do these people do in their favorite room? What are the good features of the room?

|  | *Favorite room* | *Activities* | *Good features* |
|--|-----------------|--------------|-----------------|
| Joseph Landi | ..................... | ..................... | ..................... |
| Liz Johnson | ..................... | ..................... | ..................... |
| Susan Stern | ..................... | ..................... | ..................... |

**2** Write five sentences about your favorite room.

# 8 What do you do?

## 1 WORD POWER: Jobs

**1** Identify the occupations of the people in the pictures. Use the words in the list. Then listen and practice.

| | | | |
|---|---|---|---|
| cashier | judge | pilot | security guard |
| cook/chef | lawyer | police officer | singer |
| doctor | musician | receptionist | waiter |
| flight attendant | nurse | salesclerk | waitress |

*She's a receptionist . . .*

a) *receptionist*  b) ..................  c) ..................  d) ..................  e) ..................  f) ..................

g) ..................  h) ..................  i) ..................  j) ..................  k) ..................  l) ..................

m) ..................  n) ..................  o) ..................  p) ..................  q) ..................  r) ..................

48

**2** *Pair work* Who works at the places below? Choose occupations from page 48. Add one more occupation to each list.

A: A doctor works in a hospital.
B: A nurse works in a hospital, too.

| in a hospital | in an office | in a store | in a hotel |
|---|---|---|---|
| .................................... | .................................... | .................................... | .................................... |
| .................................... | .................................... | .................................... | .................................... |
| .................................... | .................................... | .................................... | .................................... |

**3** *Class activity* Ask and answer questions about occupations.

Who . . . a) wears a uniform?
           b) stands all day?
           c) sits all day?
           d) handles money?
           e) talks to people?
           f) works hard?
           g) works at night?
           h) carries a gun?

A: Who wears a uniform?
B: Police officers wear a uniform.
C: Security guards . . .

**2** **CONVERSATION** 🔳

Listen and practice.

Rachel: Where does your brother work?
Angela: He works in a hotel.
Rachel: Oh. What does he do, exactly?
Angela: He's a chef in a French restaurant.
Rachel: That's interesting. My boyfriend works in a hotel, too.
Angela: Is he a chef?
Rachel: No, he's a security guard, but he doesn't like the work. So he's looking for a new job.

## 3 GRAMMAR FOCUS: Present tense: Wh-questions with *do* 🔲

| | | |
|---|---|---|
| Where do you work? | Where does she work? | Where do they work? |
| I work in a hotel. | She works in a store. | They work in a hospital. |
| **What do you do** there? | **What does she do** there? | **What do they do** there? |
| I'm a receptionist. | She's a cashier. | They're nurses. |

**1** Complete these sentences. Put the sentences in order to make three conversations. Listen to check your answers.

a) ........ Really? What ............... (do/does) she ............... (do/does) there?
........ She ............... (work/works) in a hospital.
........ She ............... (am/is) a doctor.
..*1*.. Where *does* (do/does) Elizabeth *work* (work/works)?

b) ........ Oh? And what ............... (do/does) you ............... (do/does) there?
........ Where ............... (do/does) you ............... (work/works)?
........ I ............... (am/is) a salesperson. I ............... (sell/sells) computers.
........ I ............... (work/works) in a department store.

c) ........ He ............... (repair/repairs) TVs.
........ What ............... (do/does) Tom ............... (do/does)?
........ He ............... (work/works) in an electronics store.
........ What ............... (do/does) he do there, exactly?

**2** *Class activity*  Ask three classmates their occupations. Then tell the class.

Where do you work?
What do you do, exactly?

"Mrs. Chen is a cashier. She works in a department store . . ."

## 4 PRONUNCIATION: Falling intonation 🔲

**1** Listen and practice.

A: Where do you work?

B: I work in a store.

A: What do you do?

B: I'm a salesclerk.

**2** Listen to the conversations again in exercise 1 of the Grammar Focus. Practice them using falling intonation.

# 5 SNAPSHOT

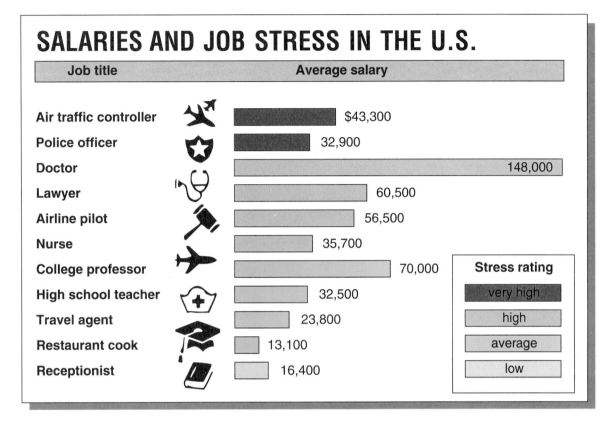

## SALARIES AND JOB STRESS IN THE U.S.

| Job title | Average salary |
|---|---|
| Air traffic controller | $43,300 |
| Police officer | 32,900 |
| Doctor | 148,000 |
| Lawyer | 60,500 |
| Airline pilot | 56,500 |
| Nurse | 35,700 |
| College professor | 70,000 |
| High school teacher | 32,500 |
| Travel agent | 23,800 |
| Restaurant cook | 13,100 |
| Receptionist | 16,400 |

**Stress rating**
- very high
- high
- average
- low

What other professions are stressful? ................................................................................................

What other professions have high salaries? ........................................................................................

# 6 CONVERSATION 🎞

Listen and practice.

Richard: Hi, Stephanie. I hear you have a new job.
Stephanie: Yes, I'm teaching math at Lincoln High School.
Richard: So how do you like it?
Stephanie: Well, the salary is a little low, but the students are nice. How are things with you?
Richard: Not bad. You know I'm an air traffic controller now.
Stephanie: Now that's an exciting job!
Richard: Yes, but it's very stressful.

51

## **7** **GRAMMAR FOCUS:** Adjectives 🔊

| **be + adjective** | **Opposites** | |
|---|---|---|
| A lawyer's salary **is high**. | high | low |
| A police officer's job **is dangerous**. | safe | dangerous |
| | interesting | boring |
| **adjective + noun** | pleasant | unpleasant |
| A lawyer has **a high salary**. | easy | difficult |
| A police officer has **a dangerous job**. | relaxing | stressful |

**1** Say it another way.

a) A nurse's job is interesting. *A nurse has an interesting job.*
b) A computer programmer's job is difficult.
c) A doctor's salary is high.
d) A lawyer's job isn't easy.
e) A chef's job is pleasant.
f) A security guard's job is dangerous.

**2** *Pair work* Complete the sentences with adjectives. Then compare answers with your partner.

a) A cashier has ............................... .
b) A salesclerk's job is ............................... .
c) A police officer's job isn't ............................... .
d) A musician has ............................... .
e) A flight attendant's job is ............................... .
f) A receptionist doesn't have ............................... .

**3** *Class activity* Find two jobs for each category. Do you and your classmates agree?

| *an exciting job* | *a high salary* |
|---|---|
| .......................... | .......................... |
| .......................... | .......................... |
| *a difficult job* | *a dangerous job* |
| .......................... | .......................... |
| .......................... | .......................... |
| *a boring job* | *a low salary* |
| .......................... | .......................... |
| .......................... | .......................... |
| *an easy job* | *a stressful job* |
| .......................... | .......................... |
| .......................... | .......................... |

A: A doctor has an exciting job.
B: A doctor's job isn't exciting. It's stressful.
C: I agree. I think a doctor has a stressful job.

▶ **Interchange 8: The perfect job** Find out what you want in a job. Turn to page IC-11.

## 8 LISTENING 🔊

Listen to these women talk about their jobs. Number the pictures from 1 to 4.

a).........     b).........     c) .........     d).........

## 9 READING 🔊

**1** Read the article, and then complete the chart.

# What do you do, exactly?

**Anthony Duran, telephone operator**

As a directory assistance operator, I give out hundreds of telephone numbers every day. I sort of like talking to people all day. I earn around $20,000 a year. But I don't feel very secure – a lot of operators are losing their jobs because of automation. Computers do everything these days. So I'm studying to be a computer programmer at night school.

**Robert Fine, travel agent**

My clients are all business travelers. I make plane, hotel, and car reservations for them. My annual salary isn't very high – only $24,000 – but I like my job. It's pretty secure, because travel is a growing field. Also, I often travel in order to learn about cities, hotels, airlines, and tours. And when I do, everything is free – the plane tickets, the hotel rooms, etc.

**Kimberly Evans, physical therapist**

In my job, I mainly work with athletes who have sports injuries. Sometimes the athletes are famous, and that's always exciting. My salary is good – $38,000 a year – and I always have a lot of patients. Doctors are too busy to do physical therapy these days, and they're happy to give the work to specialists like us.

| *Job* | *Salary* | *What they do* | *One good thing about the job* |
|-------|----------|----------------|-------------------------------|
| .................. | .................. | ........................................... | ........................................... |
| .................. | .................. | ........................................... | ........................................... |
| .................. | .................. | ........................................... | ........................................... |

**2** Write five sentences about your job, or a job you would like to have.

> I'm an accountant . . .

# Review of Units 5 – 8

## 1 Listening 📼

*Pair work*   Victoria is calling friends in different parts of the world.
Where are they? What time is it there? What are they doing? Complete the chart.

Victoria          Sue          Juan          Jim

|        | *City* | *Time* | *Activity* |
|--------|--------|--------|------------|
| *Sue*  | .................... | .................... | .................................... |
| *Juan* | .................... | .................... | .................................... |
| *Jim*  | .................... | .................... | .................................... |

## 2 Different responses

*Pair work*   Write two different answers to these questions.
Use the present continuous. Then practice with a partner.

A: What are you doing? Are you watching television?
B: No, I'm . . .

A: Are you going to school? What courses are you taking?
B: . . .

A: Is Maria at school today?
B: No, she's . . .

A: What's that noise? Is it the people in the next apartment?
B: Yes, they're . . .

A: Are you going to the party? What are you wearing?
B: . . .

## 3 | Habits

Write eight sentences about yourself. Then compare with a partner.

a) Name two things you do in the morning.
b) Name two things you don't do in the morning.
c) Name two things you do on the weekend.
d) Name two things you don't do on the weekend.

*I have breakfast in the morning . . .*

## 4 | Comparisons

*Class activity*   What are some differences between these things?
Write four sentences about each pair, using the expressions in the box.
Compare your answers with your classmates.

a) a house and an apartment
b) the city and the country

*A house has a yard, but an apartment . . .*

It has . . .
It doesn't have . . .
There is . . .
There's no . . .
There are . . .
There aren't . . .

## 5 | What's the question?

**1**   Look at these answers. What are the questions? Write the questions down.

*Where do you work?*

a) I work in a store.

b) I'm a sales clerk.

c) I really like my job.

d) I live in an apartment downtown.

e) My apartment has a kitchen, a bathroom, and a living room.

f) I need a sofa, a rug, and a carpet.

g) I think my English class is great!

i) I get up at 6:00 A.M. every morning.

j) It's four o'clock in the morning!

h) I go to class by subway.

k) I'm watching television right now.

**2**   *Pair work*   Ask and answer the questions with a partner.
Use personal information.

# Interchange Activities

## Interchange 1 | Directory Assistance – STUDENT A

*Role play*

**1** You need the telephone numbers of these people. Student B is the telephone operator. You are the customer. Follow the conversation:

| | number |
|---|---|
| Ms. Kumiko Roku | ............................. |
| Ms. Ada Rodrigues | ............................. |
| Mr. Marc Rudolph | ............................. |
| Mr. Paul Rosen | ............................. |

Operator: Directory Assistance.
Customer: I need the number of ........................... .
Operator: How do you spell the last name?
Customer: ..................................... .
Operator: And the first name?
Customer: ..................................... .
Operator: Thank you. The number is ........................... .

**2** Now you are the telephone operator. Student B needs some telephone numbers. Find the numbers in the "directory." Give the numbers to Student B.

---

### 375      DIRECTORY

| | | | |
|---|---|---|---|
| CAPUTO, Anthony | 555-4667 | CHANG, Ming Li | 555-0215 |
| CAPUTO, Frank | 555-9873 | CHRISTIE, Robert | 555-9807 |
| CARDENA, Rafael | 555-8614 | CHRISTO, Rolf | 555-7546 |
| CARDENAS, Ramon | 555-8654 | COHEN, Andrea | 555-4089 |
| CHANG, Min Li | 555-0396 | COHN, Andrew | 555-2390 |

## Interchange 2   Find the differences

**1** *Pair work*   How are the two pictures different? Ask questions to find the differences.

A: Where are the sunglasses?
B: In picture A, they're on . . .
A: In picture B, they're . . .

**2** *Class activity*   Talk about the differences with your classmates.

"In picture A, the sunglasses are on . . . . In picture B, they're . . ."

## Interchange 1 | Directory Assistance – STUDENT B

### Role play

**1** You are the telephone operator. Student A is the customer. Student A needs some telephone numbers. Find the numbers in the "directory." Follow this conversation:

Operator: Directory Assistance.
Customer: I need the number of ............................. .
Operator: How do you spell the last name?
Customer: ............................. .
Operator: And the first name?
Customer: ............................. .
Operator: Thank you. The number is ....................... .

**DIRECTORY**     1180

| | |
|---|---|
| ROCHE, Annette | 555-8125 |
| RODRIGUES, Ada | 555-9012 |
| RODRIGUEZ, Ana | 555-6734 |
| ROKU, Kumiko | 555-1392 |
| ROSE, Pearl | 555-2516 |
| ROSEN, Paul | 555-3519 |
| RUDOLF, Karl | 555-3418 |
| RUDOLPH, Marc | 555-0926 |
| RUSSO, Antonio | 555-6775 |

**2** Now you are the customer and Student A is the telephone operator. Ask for the numbers of these people:

| | *number* |
|---|---|
| Ms. Min Li Chang | ............................. |
| Mr. Rolf Christo | ............................. |
| Miss Andrea Cohen | ............................. |
| Mr. Rafael Cardena | ............................. |

## Interchange 4 | What's the weather like?

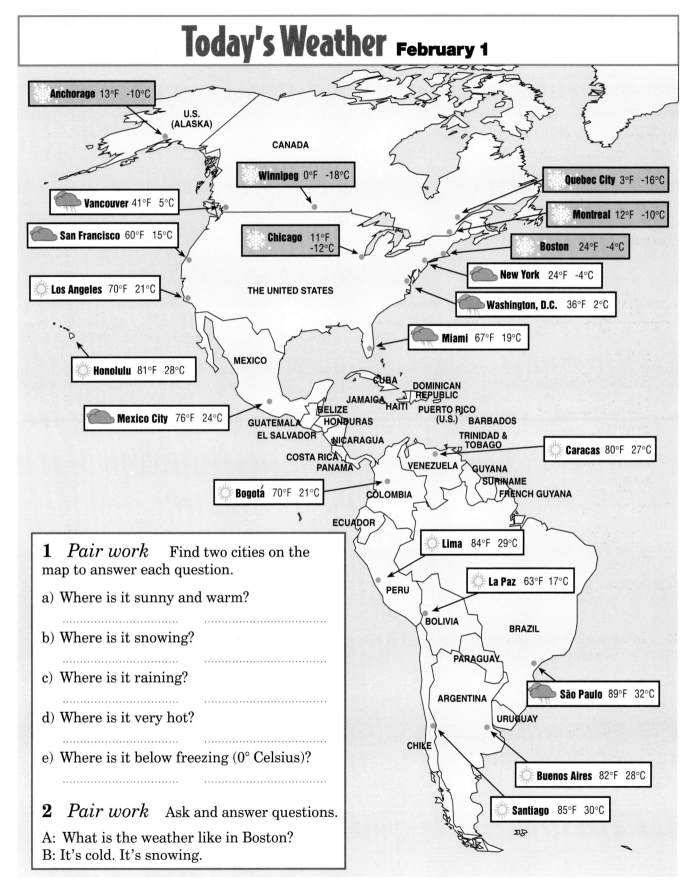

**Today's Weather** February 1

Anchorage 13°F -10°C
U.S. (ALASKA)
CANADA
Winnipeg 0°F -18°C
Quebec City 3°F -16°C
Vancouver 41°F 5°C
Montreal 12°F -10°C
San Francisco 60°F 15°C
Chicago 11°F -12°C
Boston 24°F -4°C
Los Angeles 70°F 21°C
THE UNITED STATES
New York 24°F -4°C
Washington, D.C. 36°F 2°C
Miami 67°F 19°C
Honolulu 81°F 28°C
MEXICO
CUBA
DOMINICAN REPUBLIC
JAMAICA HAITI
PUERTO RICO (U.S.)
BARBADOS
Mexico City 76°F 24°C
BELIZE
GUATEMALA HONDURAS
EL SALVADOR
NICARAGUA
TRINIDAD & TOBAGO
COSTA RICA PANAMA
VENEZUELA GUYANA
Caracas 80°F 27°C
SURINAME
FRENCH GUYANA
Bogotá 70°F 21°C
COLOMBIA
ECUADOR
Lima 84°F 29°C
PERU
La Paz 63°F 17°C
BOLIVIA
BRAZIL
PARAGUAY
São Paulo 89°F 32°C
ARGENTINA
URUGUAY
CHILE
Buenos Aires 82°F 28°C
Santiago 85°F 30°C

**1** *Pair work*   Find two cities on the map to answer each question.

a) Where is it sunny and warm?
.......................   .......................

b) Where is it snowing?
.......................   .......................

c) Where is it raining?
.......................   .......................

d) Where is it very hot?
.......................   .......................

e) Where is it below freezing (0° Celsius)?
.......................   .......................

**2** *Pair work*   Ask and answer questions.

A: What is the weather like in Boston?
B: It's cold. It's snowing.

# Interchange 3 Geography quiz

**1** *Pair work* Work with a partner to find the answers.

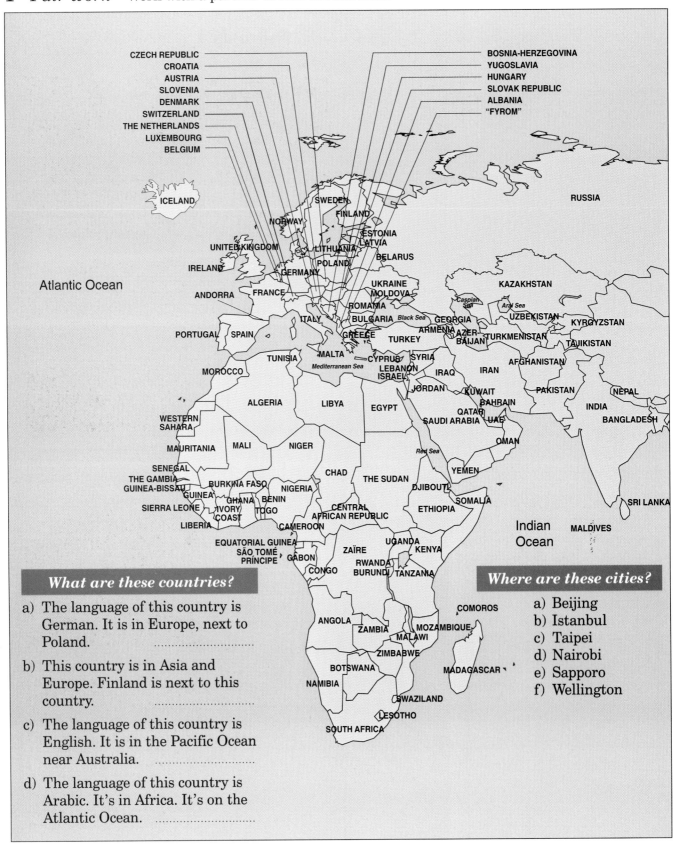

**What are these countries?**

a) The language of this country is German. It is in Europe, next to Poland. ...................

b) This country is in Asia and Europe. Finland is next to this country. ...................

c) The language of this country is English. It is in the Pacific Ocean near Australia. ...................

d) The language of this country is Arabic. It's in Africa. It's on the Atlantic Ocean. ...................

**Where are these cities?**

a) Beijing
b) Istanbul
c) Taipei
d) Nairobi
e) Sapporo
f) Wellington

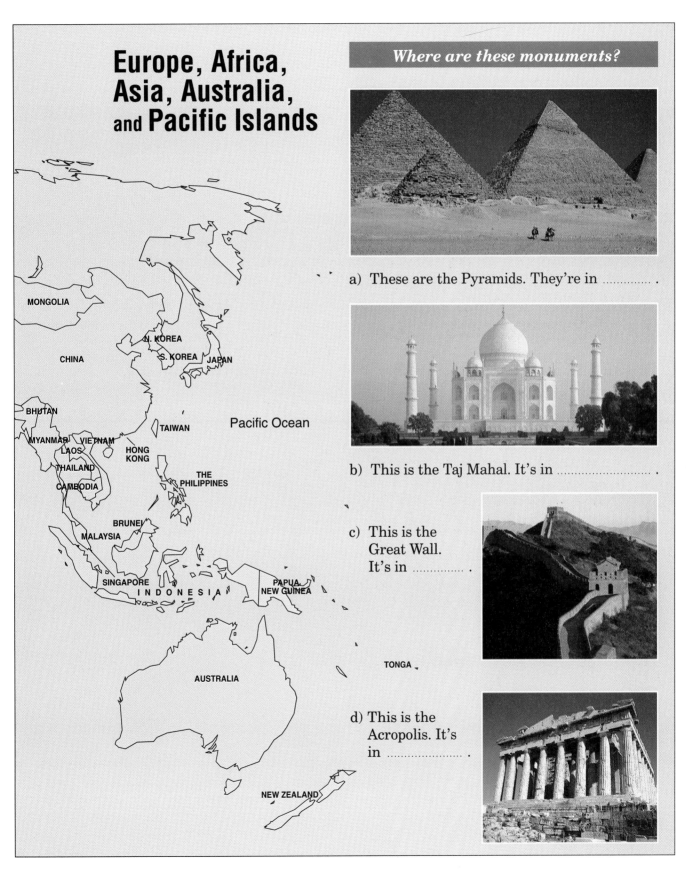

# Europe, Africa, Asia, Australia, and Pacific Islands

MONGOLIA

CHINA

N. KOREA

S. KOREA

JAPAN

BHUTAN

TAIWAN

Pacific Ocean

MYANMAR

VIETNAM

LAOS

HONG KONG

THAILAND

CAMBODIA

THE PHILIPPINES

BRUNEI

MALAYSIA

SINGAPORE

INDONESIA

PAPUA NEW GUINEA

AUSTRALIA

TONGA

NEW ZEALAND

**Where are these monuments?**

a) These are the Pyramids. They're in .............. .

b) This is the Taj Mahal. It's in .......................... .

c) This is the Great Wall. It's in ............... .

d) This is the Acropolis. It's in ..................... .

**2** *Group work*  Compare your answers with another pair.

## Interchange 5  Time zones

*Pair work*  Ask and answer questions about the cities below. Use expressions from the box.

A: What time is it in Los Angeles?
B: It's 4:00 A.M.  (It's four o'clock in the morning.)
A: What are people doing?
B: They're sleeping.

| | | |
|---|---|---|
| sleeping | working | having dinner |
| getting up | having lunch | watching |
| getting dressed | going home | television |
| going to work | shopping | |

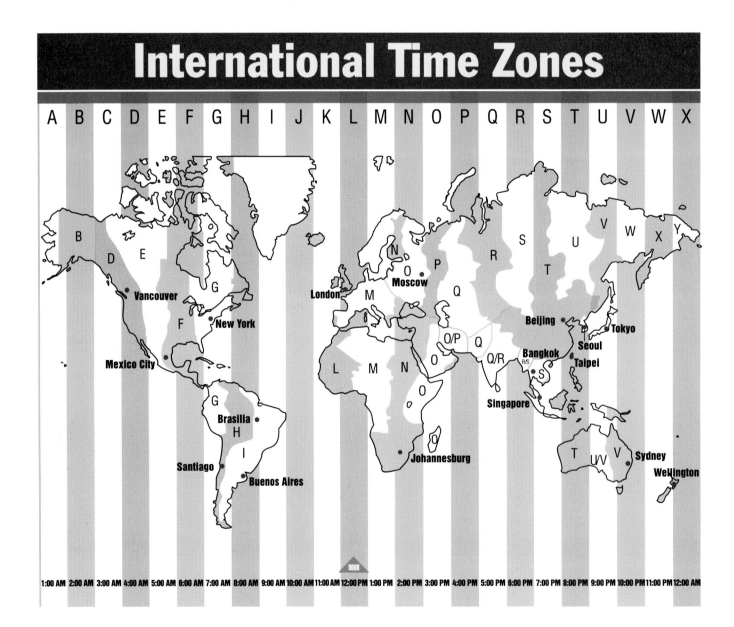

# Interchange 6 | Class survey

**1** *Class activity* Find at least one person in the class who does these things.

A: Do you get up at 5:00 A.M.?
B: No, I don't get up at 5:00 A.M.
   I get up at 7:00 A.M.

A: Do you get up at 5:00 A.M.?
C: Yes, I get up at 5:00 A.M. every day.

**2** *Class activity*
Tell the class about the
students you talk to.

A: Juan and Keiko work at night.
B: Celia works at night, too.

## Find someone who . . .

**Name**

. . . gets up at 5:00 A.M. on weekdays. ..............................

. . . gets up at noon on Saturdays. ..............................

. . . doesn't eat breakfast. ..............................

. . . has breakfast in bed. ..............................

. . . works at night. ..............................

. . . works on the weekend. ..............................

. . . lives downtown. ..............................

. . . lives in the country. ..............................

. . . lives alone. ..............................

. . . rides a bicycle to class. ..............................

. . . rides a motorcycle to class. ..............................

. . . walks to class. ..............................

. . . watches television every day. ..............................

. . . doesn't have a television. ..............................

. . . wears blue jeans every day. ..............................

. . . speaks three languages. ..............................

*riding a motorcycle to class*

*having breakfast in bed*

## Interchange 7 Find the differences

*Pair work* Write down five differences between Bill's apartment
and Jane's apartment. Then compare with your partner.

## Jane's Apartment

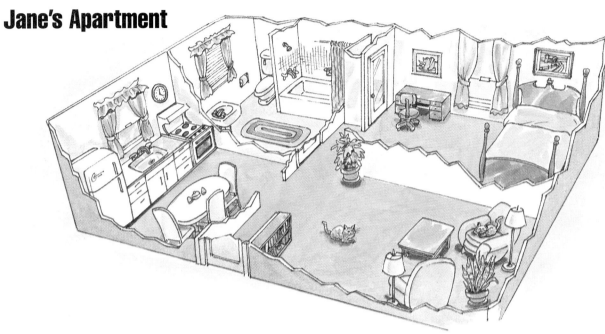

## Bill's Apartment

There are four chairs in Bill's kitchen. There are three chairs in Jane's kitchen.

There's a sofa in Bill's living room, but there's no sofa in Jane's living room.

## Interchange 8 The perfect job

**1** *Pair work* You're looking for a job. Which of these things do you want in a job? Answer the questions. Then ask your partner the same questions.

### Job Survey

| Do you want to . . . | Me Yes | Me No | My partner Yes | My partner No |
|---|---|---|---|---|
| a) talk to people? | ☐ | ☐ | ☐ | ☐ |
| b) help people? | ☐ | ☐ | ☐ | ☐ |
| c) perform in front of people? | ☐ | ☐ | ☐ | ☐ |
| d) work from 9 to 5? | ☐ | ☐ | ☐ | ☐ |
| e) make your own schedule? | ☐ | ☐ | ☐ | ☐ |
| f) use a computer? | ☐ | ☐ | ☐ | ☐ |
| g) use the telephone? | ☐ | ☐ | ☐ | ☐ |
| h) work outdoors? | ☐ | ☐ | ☐ | ☐ |
| i) work in an office? | ☐ | ☐ | ☐ | ☐ |
| j) have a private office? | ☐ | ☐ | ☐ | ☐ |
| k) work at home? | ☐ | ☐ | ☐ | ☐ |
| l) travel? | ☐ | ☐ | ☐ | ☐ |
| m) have a high salary? | ☐ | ☐ | ☐ | ☐ |
| n) speak English? | ☐ | ☐ | ☐ | ☐ |
| o) wear a uniform? | ☐ | ☐ | ☐ | ☐ |
| p) wear a suit? | ☐ | ☐ | ☐ | ☐ |
| q) wear blue jeans? | ☐ | ☐ | ☐ | ☐ |

*working from 9 to 5*

*working outdoors*

**2** *Class activity* Think of a good job for yourself. Then tell the class.

"I want to be a musician, because I want to . . ."

. . . work at home.

. . . perform in front of people.

. . . travel.

# Key Vocabulary

## Unit 1  Hello. My name is Jennifer Wan.

### NOUNS

**Classroom items**

board
book
cassette player
chair
desk
dictionary
envelope
eraser
map
notebook
pencil
piece of paper
table
wastebasket
workbook

**Other nouns**

boy
class
country
English
girl
math
name
number
telephone number
umbrella
word

### VERBS

am
are
is
close
find
go
open
say
see
spell
take out
write

### ADVERBS

here
there
over there

### PREPOSITIONS

in
on
to

### PRONOUNS AND CONTRACTIONS

I          I'm
you        you're
he         he's
she        she's
it         it's

### ARTICLES

a
an
the

### WH-WORD

what

### EXPRESSIONS

Excuse me.
What's your name?
My name is . . .
This is . . .
(It's) nice to meet you.
By the way . . .
How do you spell . . . ?
I'm sorry.
I think . . .
Please . . .
Thank you.
Yes. No.

**Hellos**

Hello./Hi.
Good morning.
Good afternoon.
Good evening.

### ADJECTIVES

**Possessives**

my
your
his
her

**Titles**

Mr.
Ms.
Mrs.
Miss

**Numbers 1–10**

(See page 5)

**Other**

first
last
right

**Good-byes**

Good-bye./Bye./Bye-bye.
Have a nice day.
See you tomorrow.
Good night.

## Unit 2  What's this called in English?

### NOUNS

**Personal items**

address book
book bag
briefcase
calculator
comb
eyeglass case
eyeglasses (pl)
credit card
driver's license
glasses (pl)
hairbrush
handbag
key
pen
photo
sunglasses (pl)
tissue
wallet

**Other nouns**

address
baby
bed
bedroom
cabinet
classroom
cushion
daughter
newspaper
question
remote control
sofa
teacher
television
thing

### VERBS

carry
pick up
put
watch

### ADVERBS

just
in bed
not
right there/here
tonight
very

### ADJECTIVES

different
new
ready
nice

**Possessives**

my
your
his
her
our
their

### PREPOSITIONS

behind
in
in front of
next to
on
under

### PRONOUNS

everything
this/these

### WH-WORD

where

### EXPRESSIONS

What's this called?
What are these called?
This is . . .
These are . . .
Thank you very much.
Thanks for watching . . .
Just one more question.

Let me see.
Great.
Actually. . .
Maybe . . .
I know.
I don't know.
Well . . .

# Unit 3  Where are you from?

## NOUNS

### Countries*

Argentina
Australia
Austria
Bolivia
Brazil
Cambodia
Canada
Chile
China
Colombia
Costa Rica
Cuba
the Dominican Republic
Ecuador
Egypt
England
France
Germany
Guatemala
Haiti
Honduras
Hungary
India
Indonesia
Ireland
Italy
Japan
Korea
Laos
Lebanon
Malaysia
Mexico
the Netherlands
Nicaragua
Nepal
New Zealand
Panama
Paraguay
Peru
the Philippines
Poland
Portugal
Russia
Spain
Sudan
Sweden
Turkey
Uruguay
the United Kingdom
the United States
Venezuela
Vietnam

## ADJECTIVES

### Nationalities*

Argentinian
Australian
Austrian
Bolivian
Brazilian
Cambodian
Canadian
Chilean
Chinese
Colombian
Costa Rican
Cuban
Dominican
Ecuadorian
Egyptian
English
French
German
Guatemalan
Haitian
Honduran
Hungarian
Indian
Indonesian
Irish
Italian
Japanese
Korean
Laotian
Lebanese
Malaysian
Mexican
Dutch
Nicaraguan
Nepalese
New Zealander
Panamanian
Paraguayan
Peruvian
Filipino
Polish
Portuguese
Russian
Spanish
Sudanese
Swedish
Turkish
Uruguayan
British
American
Venezuelan
Vietnamese

*These lists do not include all countries of the world, but do list countries that are not presented in the unit.

## NOUNS

### Regions

Africa
Asia
the Caribbean
Central America
Europe
North America
South America
the Pacific

### Other nouns

city
country
family
geography
immigrant
language

### Languages

(See page 18.)

## ADJECTIVES

good
interesting
native
official
whole

## VERBS

aren't
isn't

## ADVERBS

originally
very
now

## PREPOSITIONS

from
of
in (Spanish)

## EXPRESSIONS

Really?
Oh.
Oh, right.
Where are you from?
I'm from . . .
Here. Take it.
So . . .

# Unit 4  Clothes and weather

## NOUNS

### Clothes

bathing suit
blouse
blue jeans
boots
coat
dress
hat
high heels
pajamas
running shoes
scarf
shirt
shoes
shorts
skirt
slacks
suit
tennis shoes
tie (necktie)
T-shirt
watch (wristwatch)

### Seasons

spring
summer
fall
winter

### Other nouns

degree
taxi
temperature
weather

## ADJECTIVES

### Colors

beige
black
blue
brown
gray
green
orange
pink
purple
red
white
yellow

### Weather

cloudy
cold
cool
hot
humid
sunny
warm
windy

### Other adjectives

dark
light
Celsius
Fahrenheit

### Numbers 11–100

(See page 25.)

## VERBS

drive
play (tennis)
rain
run
snow
swim
take (a taxi)

take (a walk)
walk
wear

## ADVERBS

really
today

## PREPOSITION

below (zero)

## CONJUNCTIONS

and
but
so

## WH-WORD

What color

## EXPRESSIONS

Uh-oh.
What's the matter?
Great idea.
Come on!
Let's . . .
What color . . . ?
What's the weather like?

# Unit 5  What are you doing?

| NOUNS | VERBS | ADVERBS | PREPOSITIONS |
|---|---|---|---|

**NOUNS**

*Meals*
breakfast
lunch
dinner

*Other nouns*
clock
coffee
conference
dish
movie
television (TV)
week
work

**VERBS**

attend
call
clean (the house)
dance
get dressed
get up
have breakfast,
   lunch, dinner
go (to the movies)
go (to work)

remember
shop
sit
sleep
stay (in bed)
vacuum
wash (the dishes)
watch (television)
work

**ADVERBS**

*Times*
at night
in the afternoon
in the evening
in the morning
on Saturday
this month
this week

*Clock time*
A.M./P.M.
midnight
noon
at noon
o'clock

**PREPOSITIONS**

after
at
to

**CONJUNCTION**

if

**WH-WORDS**

what time
who
why

**ADJECTIVE**

awake

**EXPRESSIONS**

Hey!
Of course.
See you at . . .
That's OK.
I'm calling from . . .
(Do you) remember?

What time is it?
It's . . . o'clock.
It's a quarter after/to . . .
It's . . . minutes after/to . . .
. . . right?

# Unit 6  How do you go to work?

**NOUNS**

*Days of the week*
Sunday
Monday
Tuesday
Wednesday
Thursday
Friday
Saturday

*Family*
brother
child
children *(pl)*
daughter
father
husband
mother
parent
sister
son
wife

*Places*
apartment
city
country
house
park
restaurant
school
suburbs

*Transportation*
bus
car
ferry
subway
tow truck
train

*Other nouns*
job
people *(pl)*
ride
work

**VERBS**

come
do (work)
get (=pick up)
go
have (a ride)
hope
leave (for)
live
meet
need
read
serve
sleep in
speak
take (a break)
take (the bus,
   subway)
use
wait (for)
work (=function)

**ADVERBS**

*Places*
downtown
home
in the city
in the country
in the suburbs

*Times*
early
every day
every morning
late
on Sundays
on Mondays
all day
not too early
at (nine) o'clock
at midnight
at noon
on weekdays
on the weekend
on weekends

*Other adverbs*
by bus, subway
together
too (not too early)

**ADJECTIVES**

alone
big
lucky
public
retired

**PREPOSITIONS**

like
near
with

**PRONOUNS**

both
me
us

**WH-WORD**

how

**EXPRESSIONS**

a lot of
OK.
Sure.
That's good.
What about you?
You're lucky!

# Unit 7  Does the apartment have a view?

## NOUNS

### Homes/Rooms
apartment
basement
bathroom
bedroom
closet
dining room
family room
garage
house
kitchen
living room
room
swimming pool
view (of)
yard

### Furniture
armchair
bed
bookcase
chair
clock
coffee table
computer
desk
dresser
lamp
microwave oven
mirror

picture
refrigerator
rug
sofa
stove
table
television

### Other
help
neighbor
river
yard sale

## VERBS
move in
need

## ADVERBS
only
next weekend

## ADJECTIVES
some
any

## WH-WORDS
How many
What else

## EXPRESSIONS
Guess what!
No problem.
What else . . . ?
What is . . . like?

That sounds great.
Right.
Of course.
There's . . .

There are some . . .
There's no . . .
There aren't any . . .

# Unit 8  What do you do?

## NOUNS

### Jobs/Professions
accountant
airline pilot
air traffic controller
athlete
cashier
chef
college professor
(restaurant) cook
doctor
flight attendant
judge
lawyer

musician
nurse
police officer
receptionist
salesclerk
salesperson
security guard
singer
teacher
travel agent
waiter
waitress

### Other nouns
boyfriend
computer
department store
electronics store
gun
hospital
hotel
money
office
salary
store
uniform

## VERBS
agree
handle
hear
look (for)
repair
sell
sit
stand
teach
talk

## ADVERBS
exactly
really
too

## ADJECTIVES
boring
dangerous
difficult
easy
exciting
high
interesting

low
pleasant
relaxing
safe
stressful
unpleasant

## WH-WORD
Who

## EXPRESSIONS
How do you like it?
How are things with you?
Not bad.
I hear . . .
Now that's . . . !